Best of Wrestling
from
The Coaching Clinic

Best of Wrestling
from
The Coaching Clinic

Compiled by
the Editors of
The Coaching Clinic

Parker Publishing Company, Inc.
West Nyack, New York

Library of Congress Cataloging in Publication Data

Main entry under title:

Best of wrestling from the Coaching clinic.

   1. Wrestling coaching--Addresses, essays,
lectures. I. The Coaching clinic.
GV1196.3.B47   796.8'12'07   78-1462
ISBN 0-13-074898-6

Printed in the United States of America

How This Book Will Help
Your Wrestling Program

Over the years, *The Coaching Clinic* has been proud to publish many fine articles by numerous outstanding Wrestling coaches covering every aspect of the sport.

Now, in response to many inquiries and requests from Wrestling coaches around the country, we have selected what we consider to be the cream of the crop—35 outstanding articles that cover every aspect of coaching Wrestling.

In these pages, some of the nation's most knowledgeable and successful high school and college coaches provide you with a one-stop ready reference on the whole Wrestling spectrum—from program tips to drills and all points in between.

No matter how long you've been coaching Wrestling, you'll return time and time again to this invaluable anthology for tips on performance techniques, conditioning, practice schedules—even on scouting and promotional ideas.

In all, you'll find this an indispensable addition to your professional library.

The Editors of *The Coaching Clinic*

Contents

Part II
PINNING AND TAKEDOWNS

Part III
COUNTERING, ESCAPES AND REVERSALS

Part IV
PRACTICE SESSIONS

Part V
CONDITIONING AND TRAINING

Part VI
WRESTLING DRILLS

Best of Wrestling
from
The Coaching Clinic

Part I

Program Tips

1

The Beginning Wrestling Coach and His Program

by Roger D. Wilson

**Head Wrestling Coach
Issaquah High School
Issaquah, Washington**

In 15 years of coaching wrestling at Issaquah High School, Roger Wilson has compiled a win-loss record of 185-42. He has coached 12 league champions, a state champion, and his boys have placed in the top 10 at state meets eight times. His total individual champions coached at all levels—sub-region, region, and state—equals 85 at this writing.

The Beginning Wrestling Coach
and His Program

When you sign your first contract to coach high school wrestling, you have before you a very rewarding job. However, there are problems as well as rewards. The purpose of this article is to aid the beginning coach with the problems of starting his program.

NOTE: Following are a few of the methods and ideas we have found successful in our program. Although primarily intended for the beginning coach, they may be modified for use by all coaches.

School administration relationship: Of utmost importance to the beginning coach is his relationship with the school administration—especially with the principal and athletic director since they are in charge of the school and its athletic policies. It's the coach's job to know the policies of the administration regarding his program and adjust to them. Also, the coach should inform the administration of his objectives and procedures, as well as any problems that may occur.

NOTE: By establishing rapport through cooperation, the coach will find that wrestling will be accepted and treated accordingly concerning budgets, schedules, and other areas vital to a growing sport.

The coach's relationship with the other members of the faculty should be one of mutual understanding and cooperation. He must be sympathetic to their programs and policies and should, whenever possible, support them. Other areas that are to be considered for gaining faculty support are: (1) attend faculty meetings; (2) respect their discipline measures and grading policies; (3) don't ask for exceptions from duty because you are a coach.

Primary objective: What is to be considered of primary importance in the establishment of a wrestling program is entirely dependent upon the desired goals of the coach. His ideas of a program will differ from those of others—and he, as well, will change from season to season as the team develops and progresses toward the desired ends.

The primary objective should be to gain the confidence of the team and squad members. This is accomplished through words and actions—and knowledge of the sport. A coach who admits he doesn't know, yet shows his interest and concern, will fare better than an NCAA champ who is not interested. Interest is catching—and if the coach radiates interest and enthusiasm, his team in turn will be interested and motivated to do well.

Organization: Organization begins right now. A target-date calendar, with all the important items to be accomplished noted, should be prepared in advance of actual training and the season. The calendar might include a coaching clinic, workshops, summer camps, repair of equipment, purchasing equipment, school-wide recruiting, pre-season training, official turnouts, first dual meet, toughest dual meet and, finally, tournaments.

According to the schedule, the coach must make every effort to improve himself as well as the program. This is done by reading various coaching and physical education journals, books devoted to wrestling, and books concerning coaching in any related field. If the coach allots himself time to read widely, he will be able to find ideas that can be adapted to wrestling.

EXAMPLE: An example of this is the use of various track and cross-country training methods for both in-season and pre-season training for wrestling. Through reading, the coach can avail himself of new exercises, research on weight control, weight training and organizational ideas. The coach who is constantly looking for new ideas will find them.

Camps and clinics: Another facet of self-improvement to supplement research and study is frequent attendance at wrestling camps and clinics. Include also general coaching clinics and physical education classes. The value of being able to watch and talk to those more experienced than you should never be overlooked. Here's a formula that I have found helpful concerning reading and attending clinics:

1. Gather together from discussion or reading as many major ideas and thoughts as possible which may be considered new and useful.
2. After careful analysis, condense the ideas to those three that you consider the most significant.
3. Record these three on notebook paper and file for future use. If you do this each time you read an article or book or attend a clinic, you will accumulate numerous ideas for future use.

Purchasing equipment: This will vary according to the athletic budget. The equipment used in wrestling can usually be listed as: (1) mats; (2) practice uniforms and equipment; (3) meet uniforms. Before purchasing any equipment, acquaint yourself with someone who has purchased such items and ask questions. Consider the grade of the items—first line, second, etc. Purchase any questionable items in small "test" quantities, considering the amount and type of abuse the item will receive.

NOTE: Last, but not least, consider the dollar cost. If you are starting a new wrestling program, your budget will probably grow in size from year to year. Don't think that you have to buy lowest cost items in order to make them go around; assume that whatever you buy will be used again next year—and that you'll be able to add to the quantity later.

The items that have to be replaced most often are practice uniforms. It is suggested that the uniform be of medium weight and cost. The complete uniform consists of a jersey, tights, knee pads and head gear. A jersey with ¾ length raglan sleeves will withstand tug and strain better than a jersey with full length straight-shouldered seams. Knee length tights tend to wear longer because they absorb tug and strain and won't rip out in the crotch as easily as full length tights.

TIPS: Knee pads serve a double purpose: to protect the wrestler and to prolong the life of the tights. Ear guards are an essential part of the uniform in that they limit ear injuries which are the most common of all wrestling injuries.

Care of equipment: It's best to assign each wrestler a practice uniform and make him responsible for it. He must launder and repair it and turn it in at the end of the season. Placing the responsibility upon the student for the care and upkeep of his uniform minimizes loss and careless abuse. When necessary, fines are assessed for loss or excessive damage. Beyond this, the coach must assume the responsibility of cleaning and storing all equipment and uniforms. Mats must be scrubbed, disinfected, patched and stored in an area that is free from access until the following season. Equipment will give maximum use over a number of years if cared for properly.

Pre-season training: Preparation for the coming season begins near the end of summer vacation. The coach must then have his equipment orders in and be ready to start a pre-season training program. Pre-season training will vary from school to school according to administrative philosophy and local athletic regulations.

Usually, a sound pre-season training schedule should give the prospective wrestler a choice of activities. For instance, encourage as many as possible to play football—from my experience, it makes them a degree tougher, both mentally and physically. Our best dual meet record was accomplished by a team made up of football players in every weight class over 120 pounds. A second choice of training is cross-country, supplemented by a weight-training program devoted to strength building of the large muscle areas.

What to emphasize: This, too, varies from coach to coach. Some advocate vigorous conditioning all season; some emphasize mat wrestling; others stress takedowns, etc. Our philosophy is as follows:

1. Early-season: Concentrate on exercises emphasizing strength building and flexibility, standups and takedowns, quick starts from referee's position, and short rapid periods of wrestling.

2. Mid-season: Emphasis is turned to mat wrestling (rides, pins and counters), "wind" conditioning, and longer periods of wrestling.

3. Late-season: Devotion to sequence and chain wrestling, situation wrestling, and a very rigorous conditioning plan that involves long periods of wrestling alternated by running.

Weight training: Consideration should also be given to a modified weight training program which involves a minimum of time, equipment and organization. Four basic lifts constitute our weight training program—clean and jerk, military press, curls and squats. Each lift is performed with a 40-pound barbell; each exercise is done in two parts. The first part consists of a 10-second isometric contraction, followed by repetitions of the lift for 30 seconds.

> NOTE: Organize the squad into groups of three, instructing them as to the form and purpose of each lift. The isometric portion of each exercise requires participation of all three boys in a single group. Two boys position themselves at opposite ends of the barbell. The third boy performs the prescribed lift.

When the first repetition is completed about halfway, the boys at the ends of the barbell apply resistance, making the bar immovable. The "lifter" fights the resistance for 10 seconds, after which the exercise is repeated as many times as possible in 30 seconds. Total time spent on each exercise per boy is 40 seconds. This means that by rotating the members of each group, a squad of 30 using 10 barbells can complete the four lifts in 10 minutes (Figures 1 and 2).

Figure 1

Figure 2

2

A Complete
Wrestling Program

by Joe Gilas

Head Wrestling Coach
Adams City High School
Commerce City, Colorado

Joe Gilas' 12-year record as head wrestling coach at Adams City High School is 208-29-2, and includes nine league championships, seven district championships, and one state championship. His squads also have a five-year perfect dual-match record and have won eight invitational tournaments since 1960. He has had several Coach-of-the-Year awards.

A Complete Wrestling Program

No one has a corner on fundamentals and holds in wrestling. These things can be found in any book on the market—and each wrestling coach has his own bag of holds (or tricks). So it goes with wrestling (or any other sport). Therefore, there are other variables that must be uncovered to make a program successful.

NOTE: At Adams City (Commerce City, Colorado) High School, we have concentrated on a "system" of wrestling that we began some years ago. Having had little success with just a high school program, a district-wide program was initiated in all of the elementary schools—from the first-grade level through the sixth grade. We call this phase one. Phase two is our junior high program; phase three is our high school program.

This we call a complete wrestling program, and this is how it works.

PHASE ONE

In phase one we break up the elementary grades into two groups. The program here is designed to develop an interest in wrestling and to create a desire to participate. At this age level, it takes a lot of work to keep their interest at a high level and still teach them some very basic maneuvers.

Group I—grades 1, 2, and 3—meets every Saturday morning for eight weeks, from 9:00 until 12:00. The basic wrestling is interspersed with tumbling and other games to coordinate with the fundamentals being taught in wrestling.

> NOTE: The fundamentals being—a double-leg takedown with a fake; a simple breakdown and an escape; a half-nelson crotch pin; and lots of balance work. All these activities are introduced by a variety of wrestling games and drills taught by members of the high school wrestling squad.

Group II consists of the fourth, fifth, and sixth graders. They meet three days a week after school for five weeks with two high school wrestlers in charge—usually a senior boy serves as an instructor and an underclassman is his assistant.

> NOTE: This arrangement serves a double purpose. The high school boys have the knowledge of all facets of our program and are instructed in the fundamentals we wish to teach at this level. They in turn learn to become better wrestlers.

Tournament: A tournament is conducted and organized into two divisions—B division: all fourth-grade students classified into 12 weights beginning with 55 lbs. through 120 lbs., and over; A division: consists of the fifth- and sixth-grade students classified under the same 12 weights.

During the tournament, each boy will wrestle three matches and regardless of the outcome will receive a ribbon for his participation. The matches in each division consist of three one-minute periods. The tournament is the culmination of the instruction time and provides a goal for both students and their high school instructors.

PHASE TWO

As the sixth-grade student moves into the junior high school, he has the choice of trying out for the basketball program or remaining in the wrestling activities—which is phase two of our program. That many remain with the wrestling program is indicated by the size of the senior high squads. The past 12 years an average of 97 boys per year have reported for the sophomore, junior varsity, and varsity squads.

PHASE THREE

When the students turn out for our high school program (phase three), we "blow much smoke." Ours is a job of psychology. We treat the mind and work on individuals—everyone being different. One hard and fast rule in the high school program is that during practice—*each coach must relate to his particular group and say something positive to each boy to build up the mental attitude.* We stress never leaving a negative thought with a lad.

SAMPLE PRACTICE SCHEDULE

The following is a sample of our practice schedule:

Conditioning: We use the hall to run laps, going up two flights of stairs and back. It takes about a minute to run a lap and we run as many as 30 a day. We also do five minutes of isometrics, about 15 seconds per exercise.

NOTE: Forced calisthenics are most helpful—push-ups, sit-ups, running in place (all supervised under stop-watch conditions). Later on we add buddy calisthenics.

Drills: We employ several basic drills on fundamentals that are appropriate for our type of wrestling.

Situations: We work on trouble situations—positive moves converting trouble to advantage.

Workouts: We work on one of the takedown series. Early in the season, we have the boys working in groups of four according to their weights. While they are learning a particular series of takedowns, one boy will be passive and the other aggressive until they become familiar with the holds and techniques.

Next we have them working in groups of three—two boys working while the third is coaching and watching to help with maneuvers. These periods will last 30 seconds, and then the boy who is coaching will be a wrestler and one of the wrestlers will assume the coaching chores.

NOTE: We always try to mix up workouts so as to eliminate boredom.

EARLY-SEASON WORKOUT

An example of an early-season workout on takedowns (offense) is shown in Chart I.

	Tie-Up Spots	Fakes and Setups	Attack Points
1.	Wrists	pull down and go for	(single or double
2.	Elbows	pull away and go for	leg and fireman
3.	Wrist and elbow	push in and away, and go	roll)
4.	Wrist and neck	touch and go	
5.	Elbow and neck	pull one down and other up	

Chart I

Once at the point of attack (double legs), the wrestler may find himself on his knee or knees. Should this occur, we use a set of drills called "trip-flip and sit," which goes something like this—the boy shoots his takedown for a double leg and finds himself short. But he still has his arms around the opponent's legs or leg. The boy on his knees draws himself as close up to his opponent as possible, head up and to the side of the opponent. If on his knees, he slides them up to the toe of the opponent, hunches his back slightly, and then takes the body signal from his opponent as to which maneuver he will complete.

Flip: If the opponent leans on him heavily and tries to cross-face him, the wrestler will flip him up and away from his head by using the opponent's own weight against himself.

Trip: Opponent begins to back away quickly, trying to get out. The wrestler trips him backward by pressing into opponent and encircling his leg as he is going backward.

Sit: If the defensive wrestler has weight on the attacking wrestler and has him completely off-balance, the countermove is to hang on with one hand, sit under and through opponent, and bring him down while slipping behind him.

NOTE: Naturally, there are many maneuvers such as these that can be used for drills to correct mistakes.

"BLOWING SMOKE"

Feed the mind every day with positive thoughts until the boy's image of himself is very positive. He must know how you, as his coach, feel about winning—whether you are merely giving it lip service or are very sincere about it.

NOTE: He must respect you enough so that he will want to win for you, and if he loses he will feel badly enough to apologize to you for losing. This rapport between you and the individual wrestler must be developed by working at it, and yet not forcing the issue.

Be flexible: As a coach, be flexible. If the schedule which you made beforehand doesn't seem to be doing the enthusiastic job you wanted it to do, then be able to switch and fit the atmosphere of the group by changing or altering your workout.

Keep it fun: Hard work and fun can be combined at the same time. Put in competitive games to create an atmosphere of competition—while still working hard. When interest seems to lag on a particular workout or drill, or if it's late in the season—liven things up with a new drill or change over to free style or another form of wrestling.

Be positive: Be positive in everything you do in the practice room or else don't show up. Let it be known to the kids and the other coaches that you want only winners in the room.

We teach the boys to "take 'em down and pin 'em." We do not stress negative wrestling, riding the legs, or perfecting a ride. The boys will learn this style of wrestling soon enough on their own; therefore, we never practice rides.

NOTE: However, some years this will backfire when you have a weak team. But over the years, an aggressive team pays off. Teach aggression—anyone can become a defensive wrestler.

3

A Middle School Wrestling Program

by Lloyd Benjamin

Head Wrestling Coach
Fairhaven Middle School
Bellingham, Washington

Lloyd Benjamin has been coaching wrestling at Fairhaven Middle School for seven years. The high school has been undefeated in league competition in wrestling for two years—and at the new high school, a junior went to the state meet and finished fourth. Coach Benjamin is also a state official for football, basketball, and wrestling.

A Middle School Wrestling Program

There is a definite need for wrestling in the middle school's (6th, 7th and 8th grades) physical education program. Wrestling is unsurpassed for the development of total physical efficiency and effective use of the whole body. It develops confidence, courage, competitiveness and enthusiasm. It has been especially tremendous with our 6th graders who had no actual physical education classes until they came to the middle school this past year.

NOTE: The age when most boys are beginning their school competitive activities finds the 6th graders full of vitality and energy, mostly lacking in competitive "spirit," but enjoying tumbling about on the mats, pushing and shoving, and just generally being active.

A good wrestling program directs this action into a program where they learn to follow orders and cooperate while developing basic moves and holds against boys their own approximate size and weight. Here's how we go about directing the program.

Introduction: In the early part of the school year, we conduct a P.T.A. wrestling program during which we acquaint the parents with the sport. We demonstrate different holds and moves and the method of scoring them. Some 20 boys in groups of 2 do the demonstrating. We also have 2 of the better 8th graders wrestle 2 rounds—one standing and one from the referee's position.

NOTE: By witnessing the boys demonstrate and by watching an actual match, the parents overcome their fear of their sons getting hurt. Thus, participation is that much better.

Lead-up activities: We use a system of "lead-up" activities throughout the early part of the school year to strengthen muscles, build endurance and wind. These activities are extras (that is, we conduct weight training indoors in bad weather and we cover regular units of soccer, football and speedball outdoors in good weather). Some of our lead-up activities follow:

1. Weight training: All the boys have a 2-week unit on weights. Sixth graders use 10 pounds of weight and build on the number of repetitions of each event, starting with 5 and working to 20. This is to build and develop muscles of the arms, shoulders, back, legs, neck and wrists.

2. Cross-country: The running is to develop the student's legs and endurance. This event is run throughout September during the last five minutes of the regular physical education class. A regular course is set out and consists of a half-mile run uphill, around the football fields, and downhill to the front of the school.

3. Circuit training: This consists of 10 events done indoors as a warmup before other units or as a lead-up to the physical fitness test given in the early part of October. The events are: bench push-ups, shuttle run, curl-ups, burpees, jump reach, rope climb, balcony run, weights, chins and dips, rope skip and peg board.

> NOTE: Students get their names on a physical fitness list if they perform a certain number of events in a certain time limit. This gives the boys a goal to aim for during the circuit training.

4. Tumbling: Starting in January, we spend five minutes as a calisthenic warmup period—using a system of constant counting aloud and a rapid variation of events, then five minutes on tumbling which consists of rolls, dives, flips, headstands, bridges, handstands, etc.

Fundamental skills: We spend four weeks on the fundamental skills of wrestling, starting in January as a physical education unit. We start beginners in the referee's position or down on the mat as studies indicate that most accidents occur when contestants are in the standing position. Some of the maneuvers we cover are as follows:

1. The boys are in groups of two kneeling on the mat (Diagram 1) while we discuss and demonstrate the proper positioning of the top and bottom man. Then we allow them to wrestle for 30 seconds. We pick out a few groups to use as demonstrators and discuss the mistakes that were made.

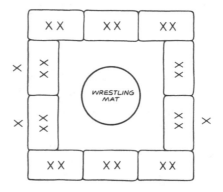

Diagram 1

EXECUTION: Two boys to each tumbling mat face the center where the instructor stands. All demonstrations are performed inside the circle of the wrestling mat. Each student has picked a classmate of his own approximate size and weight. If there are extra boys, they act as officials for the twosomes—making three boys in some groups who have to alternate.

BASIC BREAKDOWNS: We cover the basic breakdowns or controls for the top man, stressing cover of the legs, staying behind the bottom man until he has been broken down to the mat, and getting one arm of the bottom man.

2. We explain a few of the rules, the two-second count for a pin, and demonstrate the half-nelson and reverse half-nelson pinning holds, and other ways of gaining points. All the boys get a chance to break their men down to the mat and roll them over into a pinning situation. We stress getting a tight half-nelson hold, top man's chin into the armpit of the pinned man (this keeps his weight back), and body perpendicular to the bottom

man, with legs spread wide, toes down. Then we have the bottom man try to get away.

SLOW MOTION: We feel it's better to go through everything in slow motion to learn the holds correctly, then work on speed of applying the holds.

3. Escapes and reversals for the bottom man are next. We stress keeping active and moving—making the first move and keeping in action and motion. We use the same setup as before except that the bottom man starts the action, while the top man gives little opposition. Sit-outs are stressed with moves each way, then rolls and finally the standup and breakaway.

NOTE: For the first two weeks, all wrestling is done in the referee's position—increasing the amount of wrestling time of the groups to one minute's duration.

4. The use of blocks, breaks and counters for the different holds are covered after escapes and reversals are well learned. By now the students can wrestle a round of 1 to 1½ minutes and show some improvement of skills. The instructor should take his time and correct errors and mistakes as they occur. He should also praise and encourage the boys.

5. Standing takedowns are covered in one week. In slow motion, we start and teach leg trips, lifts and drops, tackles—and stress bending at the waist, keeping the head up, weight off the heels, not taking long steps or cross-over steps, keeping the elbows in and down.

IMPORTANT: It's most important that the wrestler doesn't watch the opponent's eyes. The hips and feet are more revealing. Also, the wrestler needs to remain alert when within an opponent's reach.

We use the same system as shown in Diagram 1 for the students. We demonstrate the takedown, watch the group do it, correct mistakes and go through another takedown, etc., until all are learned.

6. Once the standing takedowns are mastered by the group, we cover blocks and counters of the takedowns. We allow 2 rounds of wrestling by now, of 1½ minutes each, one standing and one round in the referee's position. These matches are more

for practice and endurance before the actual competition starts in the intramural program.

7. Mat games are used throughout the practice and learning time to break up the training sessions and provide some change of pace. Games like "king of the mountain," "war" and "up-and-down," etc., are played—plus having the whole group practice and review all material taught. This keeps everyone busy getting a good workout, and allows the instructor to pick out those boys who are most active and have the best potential.

> EXAMPLE: The game liked best is "war." All the boys are divided into two groups—red and gold. The two teams are on their knees and on different sides of the wrestling mat, facing each other. On the whistle, the boys must crawl to their opponent and wrestle him down where his shoulders are held against the mat momentarily. This puts the pinned man out while the winner can go on and help his teammates. There are many variations of good competitive workouts.

Intramural program: In the physical education classes, the 6th graders wrestle against an opponent within 10 lbs. of their weight. Winners take on winners while losers take on losers in a double-elimination tournament conducted within the class. There are certificates for the first three places in each weight class. 7th and 8th graders have winners going into an intramural program after school—taking on winners in their weight class from other physical education periods, also in a double elimination tournament.

> NOTE: Weight classes run every 10 lbs. from 65 to heavyweight (over 175). Charts are kept of the matches and posted in the gym—and also announced over our public address system every morning so that the boys know when they wrestle and against whom.

Circuit training: Our circuit training takes in the following exercises:

1. Bench push-ups: Boys place their feet on a bench and with hands on the floor do as many push-ups as they can with no breaks or stops. When they feel that they can't do another one, they must hold their body up—hands on the ground, feet on the bench, back straight—until the minute is completed. Thirty push-ups get a 6th grader on the wrestling club.

2. *Shuttle run:* This consists of the boys starting at the mid-court line of the basketball court. On the whistle, they run to the end line of the basketball court, touch the line and run back again retouching the line. This is continued for the full minute. To get on the club, a boy must do fifteen laps.

3. *Curl-ups:* This is like a sit-up but the student's legs are bent, hands are behind the head with the fingers interlocked. The chest must come upright to touch the bent legs or at least perpendicular with the floor. Forty-five curl-ups are needed to get on the club.

4. *Burpees:* The students are standing and on the whistle they start by dropping into a squat position, throw their legs back into a push-up position, then back to the squat and up. This counts as one burpee; it takes 30 to get on the club.

5. *Jump reach:* This event is done by having the student line up along a wall and jump upwards reaching first with the right hand to the greatest height he can reach—then repeat with the left hand. This is continued for one minute.

> NOTE: To get on the jump reach club, the student must stand against a wall, toes inward touching the wall, and hands overhead as far as they will reach on the wall. A partner's hand in the small of the back makes sure that there is full reach. The test is the difference between his standing reach and his jumping reach. Fifteen inches gets a 6th grader on the club.

6. *Rope climb:* Students must climb the 20-foot rope with hands only. At the end of the school year when we run the circuit training again so students can get on the clubs, the rope climb is timed. The climb must be made in fifteen seconds.

7. *Balcony run:* This event consists of the student running up the stairs, around the balcony and back down the stairs on the other side of the gym. Twice around gets him on the club.

8. *Weights:* Students work on arm and shoulder development of weight training doing arm curls, bench presses, etc.

9. *Chins and dips:* Ten chins and sixteen dips are required to get on these clubs.

10. *Rope skip and peg board:* To get on the rope skip club, the

student must jump one hundred times without a miss in one minute. To get on the peg board club, he must be able to move the pegs up or along the twelve holes.

Follow-up: The 7th and 8th grade winners of our intramural programs become the nucleus of an All-Star team picked to wrestle All-Star teams from the other two middle schools in an interscholastic meet. The high schools have an interscholastic wrestling program for the 9th graders, a junior varsity team, and a varsity squad—while the college in town has wrestling as a major sport.

SUMMARY: Wrestling in our county and area is finding more and more participants and followers each year. Schools are adding wrestling to their physical education programs, and as a sport are finding that a good wrestling program can draw as big a crowd into a gym as other sports—and that the fans are just as enthusiastic.

4

A Wrestling Coach's Philosophy for Developing Champions

by Harry B. Gibbons

Head Wrestling Coach
Brookings High School
Brookings, South Dakota

Harry Gibbons is head wrestling coach at Brookings High School, where his seven-year record is 36-12. Besides his share of conference and regional championships, he has won three state championships.

A Wrestling Coach's Philosophy for Developing Champions

Over the years, I have come to the conclusion that the difference between a champion wrestler and just another wrestler is a combination of several factors. Here they are:

- First is the ability to explode into a move, which the coach can help develop by a process of progressive aggressiveness. An example of this is in teaching the switch. Start with the defensive wrestler using switches at one-quarter speed and hitting ten switches, increasing the speed of each successive move to a point at which the offensive wrestler cannot take the force on his arm. The offensive man must tell the defensive man when his arm is hurting.
- Second is the willingness of a wrestler to keep moving on the mat, no matter what his position is during the match. Not all moves have to be for the direct purpose of pinning his opponent. Many moves are employed merely to set up an opponent or to keep the opponent countering moves.
- Third, a champion wrestler must be able to control his opponent. Two boys of equal knowledge and reaction time will find that the strongest boy will win. But many wrestlers do not like strength work with weights because they are trying to cut weight, and weight training increases the size of muscle groups.

NOTE: I suggest workout temperatures of 80 to 85 degrees, so the boys really work to lose weight. Do not let them wear a lot of clothes. After the workout, the boys might sit around awhile in plastic suits and sweat it off.

- Fourth, a boy must have confidence in himself. He must know that he can get a reversal takedown, or get off his back if his aggressive action puts him in an undesirable position. In other words, if his move does not work, he can wrestle out of it.
- Fifth is the willingness to concentrate on simple fundamentals—usually, two moves from each position are all a good wrestler needs, and to be able to do these moves very well takes a lot of work in repeating drills and getting timing down.
- Sixth is that unknown quantity of heart or courage. This desire of not wanting to be beaten can be somewhat helped by setting up goals, using pride techniques, slogans, and the like. But if a coach can select a boy who really hurts mentally when he is beaten, I believe that boy will be his best prospect.

In conclusion, there is a very small difference between the champion and the second-place finisher, but as just one point separates them in the finals—maybe just one of these factors separates them from becoming a state champ.

5

Organization in Wrestling

by Harvey E. Weigle

**Head Wrestling Coach
Moore High School
Moore, Oklahoma**

Harvey Weigle started coaching wrestling at John Marshall High School (Oklahoma City, Oklahoma) in 1964 as an assistant. The following year, he was assigned the head coaching position. His record there was 42-11 and included three state championships and two Coach-of-the-Year awards. He is presently head wrestling coach at Moore High School. His overall record is 101-44 and includes coaching 12 individual state champions.

Organization in Wrestling

It's my belief that organization is one of the most important items for the wrestling coach to consider. I do not mean organization for daily practices alone, but organization for the entire season. I think that every coach should organize his season to some extent before it begins.

NOTE: One can always alter his plans after the season progresses—you can add more to it, if the boys need the extra work, or you can take some away.

PHILOSOPHY

I think that lesson plans are the best method for planning daily practices. In this respect, I always sit down during a free hour each day and outline on paper every detail of a particular practice. If you don't do this, you will probably forget some of the points you had intended to cover during the practice.

I always keep my lesson plans from day-to-day and from year-to-year. I am always referring to last year's lesson plans to see what we were working on at the same time the preceding season. Try as we may, all of us forget certain important coaching facts from year to year.

PHASES: My season is organized for the year into five phases. The following is a breakdown of those phases and the procedure for practice during each of these five phases.

Phase I (Sept. 1 to Oct. 15): During this period of time we don't do any actual practice. This is always a confusing period of time—with the starting of school, schedule changes, class elections, sophomore orientation, etc. At our school, and most schools with which I'm familiar, athletes are excused the last hour to participate in sports. During this period of time, I meet with the wrestlers for brief discussions.

NOTE: Some of the things we cover include—physical examinations; fees for towels (a school policy); workout procedures; weight reduction; meetings with parents; files on each wrestler; manager selection; shots; letter requirements; team tryouts; holiday and weekend schedules and policies.

Phase II (Oct. 15 to Oct. 30): During this two-week period we work mainly on conditioning—and most of it is running. It is usually warm enough so that we can run outside every day. But if it's too cold we do the running indoors.

We start by having the boys run 2 miles at a fast jog, and increase the distance a quarter of a mile each two days until we reach 4 miles. After the running, we go inside for about 20 minutes of calisthenics. After that we go back outside for sprints—usually 25 to 50 20-yard sprints, 10 to 20 50-yard sprints, and 5 to 10 100-yard sprints. We then go back inside for buddy-type calisthenics.

Phase III (Nov. 1 until after Christmas): During this period of time a typical day's lesson plan would be about as follows:

(a) *Squad meeting.* A squad meeting is held before each practice to let the boys know what we're going to do and what is expected of them. We also touch on morale, discuss problems if any, or any other item that needs attention.

(b) *Run 2 to 4 miles (usually 4)–with a time limit.*

(c) *Calisthenics (same as in Phase II).*

(d) *Drills.* Every coach usually has his particular drills that he likes. Any move or series of moves can be made into a drill. For instance, I have about 15 standard drills that we execute each day of practice.

(e) *Instruction period.* I always demonstrate or have an assistant coach demonstrate moves. As the moves are demonstrated, the wrestlers execute each move to perfect technique.

NOTE: Do not try to cover too much in one day. It is best to stress one or two moves each day. It then takes constant drilling the succeeding days before the moves are perfected.

Always vary any type of instruction. I will give instruction in takedowns for two or three days in succession; then instruction on down moves for two or three days; then pinning; control; etc. This keeps your squad from concentrating on any one phase of wrestling.

(f) *Work period.* At the first of the year, we go about ten minutes on our feet and gradually increase it until we are working 30 minutes at a time on our feet. We assign partners to make sure that each boy gets a good, fair workout. After the takedown period, I have them work on the mat for from ten to 30 minutes.

(g) *Sprints or run bleacher steps.* If it is warm enough, I still have the boys run outside—but in cold weather, it is necessary to work inside.

(h) *Showers.*

Phase IV (after Christmas until the end of the season): During this period of time, the instruction period is reduced in length. Most of the material that I teach has been covered and I have put it into drills or review it occasionally. Thus, the workouts now are about 20 minutes shorter. The team should be in pretty good shape by this time.

NOTE: If there are individuals who are not in shape, I work with them. The same applies to boys who are behind on their moves or a phase of wrestling.

Phase V (end of season until school closes): After the season is over, the boys get a couple of weeks of rest. Then we start on weight lifting. We specialize on legs, arms, back, etc. —whatever a wrestler needs most. This period of time is also good for special activities, such as learning to rope climb, walk on hands or any other device that may help the wrestling program.

CONCLUSION

That's our wrestling program. As we see it, a wrestling coach needs to be highly organized. Both his daily workouts and his entire season need to be carefully planned.

6

Developing the "Thinking Wrestler"

by Neil Pietrangeli

**Former Head Wrestling Coach
Pio Nono High School
Milwaukee, Wisconsin**

Neil Pietrangeli was a wrestler at Notre Dame, captain of the team, and MVP for the 1965-66 season before he started coaching the sport. In his last two seasons at Pio Nono High School, he posted a 21-1 mark which included a conference and a state championship. Although no longer coaching at the high school level, in his spare time away from the computer industry he's active in the Kids' Wrestling Program (grades 1-9) for Cedar Athletic Association in Eagan, Minnesota.

Developing the "Thinking Wrestler"

We believe that it takes more than the physical mastery of the various holds and techniques to become successful wrestlers. It is necessary for the athletes to develop the mental abilities to recognize and adapt to, immediately, the ever changing situations that present themselves during the course of a match. In short, to be successful one must become a "thinking wrestler."

NOTE: To develop the thinking wrestler, we divide our program into two phases—focusing on the approach we use in our drills and on two special days in our wrestling week.

Since we get our athletes without benefit of exposure to wrestling prior to entering ninth grade, we strive to have them advance to the second phase of the program as soon as possible. My assistant, Thomas Knitter, is in complete charge of the first phase of the program. It is his judgment that most influences when a boy is ready to advance to our second phase.

FIRST PHASE

The first phase of our program includes mainly those wrestlers in the ninth and tenth grades. These boys are taught all of the basic holds of the sport and the drills we use to develop correct reactions to the different situations in a match. They are also given a working knowledge of the rules of wrestling.

NOTE: It's most necessary for the athletes to become familiar with the rules of wrestling to avoid the unnecessary loss of match points through penalty situations—also to give them a secure foundation for what they must learn and do to defeat or neutralize stronger opponents, and avoid bad situations against inferior opposition.

SECOND PHASE

The goal of the second phase of our program is to develop a wrestler who is capable of handling, mentally and physically, any situation that presents itself on the mat. One very obvious point must be remembered, but very frequently is not, and that is that every boy cannot become a champion but everyone can contribute to the team.

To develop this type of wrestler, we follow the belief that we must move first and be capable of handling any counterattack that may present itself. Note here that we believe it is essential to move first and take the match away from our opponent.

Several things have contributed to the success we have had with the second phase of our program:

• The utilization of our seniors to teach and assist the younger boys in the development of their skills. In the early part of the season, we pair our seniors with the least experienced wrestlers in our group, especially when executing our drills. Also, we call upon the seniors to spend extra time with the younger boys before, during, and after practice.

• Our drills, which will be explained later in the article, have an approach that avoids repetition and yet accomplishes our aims.

• We believe in maximum effort during workouts. We keep the duration of our workouts to two hours or slightly less, during which time the boys are kept on the go. One of our biggest aids in accomplishing this is the elimination of rubber sweat suits, except for the running part of the workout.

• We place special emphasis on two days of our wrestling week—the day before a meet (dual or tournament) and the practice day immediately after a meet.

NOTE: The workout aspects of our second phase are fairly standard, so the remainder of this article will concentrate on our two special days of the practice week—the day before and after a meet—and our drill program.

DAY BEFORE A MEET

We consider the day before a meet the focal point for our

47

performance in the meet itself, whether a dual or tournament. We want our wrestlers to be both mentally and physically ready to accept the challenges of the next day.

To focus the attention of the wrestlers on the job they have to do, we employ a 45-minute workout, followed by a combination scouting report and situation discussion that generally lasts no more than 15 minutes. Finally, we finish with a warm-down run of about ¾ of a mile.

> NOTE: After this the boys do one of two things: shower and leave, or if they are not a minimum of ½ pound underweight, they must work until this goal is achieved. We constantly stress the need for getting to weight and maintaining it throughout the season.

The workout itself is divided into five parts, with no resting during any of the parts and as little time as possible wasted shifting from one part to another.

1. We spend 15 minutes running a mile and generally loosening up.

2. We work on takedowns with our situation approach through the use of our "go-go" drill, which will be explained later.

3. We use about 10 minutes of our "situation" drill for escapes, reversals, and breakdowns.

4. We move into 5 minutes of work on our pinning combinations.

5. We conclude the workout with either matches of 1 minute or 5 minutes' work with our "mat" drill.

DAY AFTER A MEET

Our practice on the day after a meet is usually the longest one of our week and equal in importance to our focusing on the day before a meet. On this day, we cover each individual's performance to determine what can be improved and what needs particular concentration.

To enable us to cover these individual achievements, we make use of three different charts (Charts A, A-1, B). Chart A'

Name	TD	R	E	NF	PT	F	P	TD	R	E	NF	PT	F	P	W	L	Team PN	OPP

Chart A: Individual Dual Meet

Pio Nono			
Pio Nono			
Pio Nono			
Pio Nono			

Team Dual Meet

Name	TD	R	E	NF	PT	F	P	TD	R	E	NF	PT	F	P	W	L	TEAM POINTS

Chart A-1: Individual Tournament Results (Yearly Totals)

Name	W	L	PTS	W	L	PTS	W	L	PTS	W	L	PTS	W	L	PTS	W	L	PTS

Team Tournament Results (Yearly Totals)

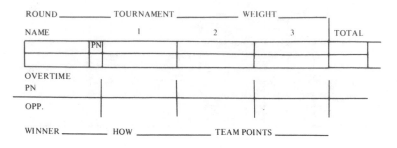

Chart B

contains the results of the single dual meet of the night before (taken directly from the scorebook) and the running total of the entire dual meet year.

For tournaments we use Chart B (a 3″ × 5″ card) to show individual matches, and Chart A-1 (which is similar to Chart A) to keep a record of the yearly totals.

> NOTE: Not only do these charts enable the coaches to evaluate performance, but also the athletes themselves are able to see how they are progressing. On these charts, we use the number of moves rather than the point values assigned to them.

Having taken care of this part of our program, we then move into a conventional practice session, concentrating most of our efforts on takedown maneuvers and counters.

DRILL PROGRAM

The drills we use are similar to those used by other coaches. The three that have proven most successful for us are described below.

Mat drill: This is used for conditioning and reactions. It is similar to the football grass drill in that it is started in the basic stance with the feet rapidly tapping on the mat. The difference is that we use commands relating to various wrestling moves.

The basic commands that we use are UP (the wrestler executes a stand-up and returns to the basic stance with his feet tapping), SPRAWL (man throws his feet back, landing on his elbows and stomach), KNEES (follows sprawl and involves bringing the elbows in tight and the knees up to the chest), BACK (wrestler falls on his back and immediately assumes a high bridge, holds for two counts, spins out, and returns to the knees position).

> NOTE: Along with these commands can be used any other terms relating to holds or specific calls. We try to build up the ability of the wrestler to do this drill until he can go for six 1-minute periods with 15 seconds' rest between periods.

Go-go drill: This we use for takedowns from changing situations. Two wrestlers face each other in their basic stance with the tips of their fingers just touching. The wrestlers may also be in any of the various tie-ups at the start of the drill. One is designated as offense and the other as defense. The coach states a takedown to be used and gives the command "go."

On the first command, the wrestlers begin tapping their feet rapidly on the mat, and while maintaining contact with each other, start moving in a circular fashion. At this time, the coach gives the command "go" a second time. Now the offensive wrestler shoots the required takedown move; the defensive wrestler is allowed one countermove. Then the offensive wrestler must block the counter, follow through, and take his opponent to the mat.

> NOTE: Once the takedown has been made, both wrestlers return immediately to the starting position and exchange roles.

There are two reasons for restricting the defensive man's mobility. One, he knows what the offensive wrestler is going to do. Two, the purpose of the drill is to work on the takedown, especially the following through of the initial move and securing the points, or at least a neutral position.

Situation drill: We use this for any series of moves on which we wish to concentrate. For example, here's the way we work on stand-ups. We use four types of stand-ups and place our wrestlers in groups of two, with one in the offensive position and the other in the defensive position. At the beginning of the season, we restrict the top man to half-speed and gradually increase to full-speed over 10 or 15 seconds of time.

Let's say the coach indicates an inside-leg stand-up. The wrestlers assume correct starting positions and are given the starting commands, "Wrestlers ready, wrestle." At the command, the bottom man executes the stand-up as quickly as he can. The top man has the choice of trying to hold him down or follow him up.

If he elects to hold him down, he may use any of the available breakdowns or may go into the back-heel block series or into the single-leg series to stop the move. If he elects to follow the man to the standing position, he may then go into the forward trip or the back trip, etc., to return his opponent to the mat.

7

Scouting as a Wrestling Coaching Technique

by Thomas E. Flanigan

**Department of Physical Education
University of Illinois
Urbana, Illinois**

Thomas E. Flanigan is a former high school wrestling coach. He is now a member of the faculty in the department of physical education at the University of Illinois. He is currently teaching advanced wrestling, which involves supervising physical education majors in the teaching of wrestling skills to the junior high school boys.

Scouting as a Wrestling Coaching Technique

In order for a wrestling coach to be effective, it is necessary for him to have as much information as possible about the opponents his wrestlers expect to face in both dual meets and tournaments. This area is often neglected or is carried on in a rather loosely organized fashion.

NOTE: An important tool for the wrestling coach then is the use of a standardized scouting report for all opponents. Such a report may take more time but can often provide the coach with the one or two additional pieces of information which may make the difference between victory and defeat.

ADVANTAGES TO WRESTLER AND COACH

The use of the scouting report and the practice of scouting opponents can be most advantageous to the individual wrestler. First of all, it gives the wrestler the obvious advantage of having concrete information about the wrestling habits and traits of his opponent so that he can prepare his own bout strategy more realistically.

Secondly, the coach himself can use the information about a prospective opponent to better prepare his practice sessions. The coach can plan practices on the basis of the strengths and weaknesses which he has identified through observations of the prospective opponents. During his scouting session, he looks for patterns of characteristics of all team members as well as those noted in individual performances.

Since wrestlers often form patterns of performance which they maintain over a long period of time, it is possible to use the scouting report as a reminder of a person's wrestling style when one is preparing for late tournament competition.

EXAMPLE: For example, when a coach prepares a wrestler for a tournament, the scouting report on a prospective opponent may serve as a useful reminder if the wrestler had met the opponent earlier in the season but had more or less forgotten his style.

Of some importance to the wrestling coach is the idea that he can often provide a psychological lift to his wrestlers if he can provide information about prospective opponents in such a way that the wrestler can feel confident that he understands his opponent, and therefore feels prepared to take advantage of weaknesses or can adequately defend against strengths.

SCOUTING REPORT INFORMATION

The information which should be recorded on the scouting report pretty much parallels the type of questions that a wrestler might ask about a prospective opponent. The wrestler is interested in knowing if his opponent is aggressive or defensive. Is the opponent fast on his feet; does he try a variety of moves; does he have one favorite move and also attempts to set up his opponent in such a way that he can work his favorite move? What kind of moves are used from the underneath positon—does he try to roll, to turn in, to sit out, to switch, or to stand up? What types of moves does he use from the top—does he go for the pin, or does he hang back and try to ride? Can the prospective opponent be characterized as a leg man and does he use the legs as a ride, or is he always looking for the pin? What counters can a wrestler expect his opponent to use?

WRESTLING SCOUTING SHEET

The answers to these and other questions can be recorded in a systematic way on a scouting sheet (Chart I) that can be

Date _____　　　　　　　　　　　　　Name _____ Weight _____

Scouted by _____　　　School _____ Opponent _____

Takedowns

Stance:	closed _____	open _____	upright _____	crouched _____	varies _____
Style:	aggressive _____	defensive _____	combination _____	fast _____	strong _____
	ties up _____	comment: _____			
Types:	double leg _____	single leg _____	duck under _____	Fireman's _____	Kelly _____
	arm drag _____	other _____			
	comment: _____				

Strong points: _____ Weak points: _____

_____　　　　　　　 _____

From Under

Moves quickly with whistle _____	waits _____	turns in _____	stands up _____	rolls _____
	sits out _____	switchs _____	short sit-out _____	clamps up _____	
	stays on base _____				
	comment: _____				

Strong points: _____ Weak points: _____

_____　　　　　　　 _____

From Top

Moves quickly with whistle _____	waits _____	legger _____	pinner _____	rides _____
	types of breakdowns _____				
	types of counters _____				
	types of rides _____				
Pinning moves:	half-nelson _____	3/4 nelson _____	cradle _____	arm bar _____	
	chicken wing _____	1/4 nelson _____	suck back _____	other _____	

General

Outstanding characteristics _____

General strengths _____

General weaknesses _____

RECOMMENDATIONS

Chart I: Wrestling Scouting Sheet

developed by the wrestling coach to serve his own needs. In developing this scouting sheet, the coach must take into consideration several factors:

1.　The scouting report should be concise and easy to read.
2.　The scouting report should be organized in general categories. For example, information about takedowns

listed in one area, with information about wrestling from underneath in another area, and wrestling in the top position listed in a separate area, etc.

3. Where possible, a checkoff system should be used in order to hold written explanations to a minimum. When scouting a wrestler involved in a fast-moving bout, it is not possible to take a lot of time for long written explanations, since the person doing the scouting may miss some of the important action.

4. The scouting report should be organized in such a way that the coach can list information on one sheet. This technique will serve two purposes. It will eliminate the need to flip pages back and forth while recording and at the same time will permit the reader (the coach, and later, the wrestler) the opportunity to scan the information without having to go from page to page. Additionally, this technique will allow the simplification of filing the information for future use.

5. A filing system should be developed by the coach in a systematic way so that the retrieval of the information can be expedited. In this regard, such a system of filing the information should take into consideration the possibility that prospective opponents may be scouted more than once during a season and for that matter, several times over the years.

6. The scouting report should also contain information about both wrestlers in a particular bout since the strategy of the wrestler may look quite different when scouted on separate occasions against different types of wrestlers.

A very useful technique for the coach is to involve his wrestlers in the process of scouting opponents. One can see the obvious value of having a wrestler personally study his prospective opponent's moves, strengths, and weaknesses. Furthermore, this practice can afford the wrestler the opportunity of seeing some wrestling moves which he may wish to add to his own style.

The coach can also use scouting as a means of studying the officials. It is possible to determine to some extent an official's techniques. For example, the coach can record how the official calls stalling, how he treats wrestling on the edge of the mat, whether or not he is fast or slow in calling takedowns and reversals, how technical he is with the referee's position, etc.

CONCLUSION

In summary, the use of scouting opponents as a coaching technique can be valuable to the operation of a successful wrestling program. The extent to which this technique is used is determined by the coach in relationship to his own program. The practice of scouting opponents can provide a means by which the coach can more adequately prepare his wrestlers for future competition.

8

Promotional Tips
for High School Wrestling

by Alex Turnamian

Head Wrestling Coach
Bergenfield High School
Bergenfield, New Jersey

Alex Turnamian has been coaching high school wrestling for ten years, nine of them as a head coach. Since coming to Bergenfield High School, he has a record of 74-23-1. His teams have won two league championships, two district championships, and two county tournaments.

Promotional Tips
for High School Wrestling

The promotion of wrestling is of vital importance to the success of your program. With the many outside interests of today's youth, the responsibilities of the wrestling coach cannot stop in the wrestling room. Today's coach must be a press agent, public relations man, recruiter, and salesman to attract the boy with athletic ability.

NOTE: Promotion of wrestling should not only be directed toward the possible candidates, but should also include the student body, the parents, and the community. Here are some promotional activities and methods that have proven successful for us.

● Conduct wrestling assemblies in the elementary and junior high schools. We take four outstanding members of our wrestling team to such gatherings where we explain the rules of the sport, the scoring system, and then demonstrate a few basic moves. We also invite everyone to the upcoming wrestling match.

● Encourage the Recreation Department to sponsor a wrestling program for youngsters. Our Recreation Department sponsors a program for boys from the fifth to eighth grades. This past season, our program involved some 160 youngsters who practiced twice a week and competed in Saturday morning matches.

● Always be available to speak at community organizational meetings, such as the Rotary Club or the Kiwanis Club. Just throw some mats in the back of your car, bring along a few of your wrestlers, and you're ready to put on a wrestling demonstration after dinner. You'd be surprised at the interest you generate—and you may even get several of the members to a few matches.

• The coaching staff should invite every boy in the school to participate in the wrestling program. Discuss with the prospective candidate the benefits of wrestling and why he should join the team. Announce over the public address system the date of the sign-up meeting for wrestling—every day for one week prior to the meeting. It helps.

• Use the public address system to remind students of matches, give them results of matches, and congratulate boys who turned in outstanding wrestling performances. Display wrestling schedules in prominent places throughout the school and community.

NOTE: Our Director of Athletics takes care of this (wrestling schedules) with the assistance of our "Mat Maids" (more about these girls later).

• Try to employ the services of cheerleaders at wrestling matches. If you can't get the varsity cheering squad, the junior varsity squad might be helpful. Better yet, try to organize your own cheerleaders exclusively for wrestling.

• Try to include a unit on wrestling in the physical education curriculum of the elementary, junior, and senior high schools. It would be a good idea for the wrestling coach to write up a course of study for the various grade levels and perhaps have an in-service training day with all physical education instructors.

• Express and show interest in other programs of the school and you will find these people attending your wrestling matches. For example, our coaches have chaperoned various activities of our high school band—and consequently, we have many members of the band on our wrestling team. Also, some of the girls in the band have joined our Mat Maids organization.

• Start a Mat Maid Club. We initiated this in our school about two years ago and it has developed into a highly successful organization. It is composed of girls who have a sincere interest in the wrestling program. Their primary responsibility is the promotion of wrestling in the school and community. Some of their activities include the following:

NOTE: (1) Scorekeepers; (2) tournament work; (3) produce and distribute programs; (4) maintain scrapbook; (5) sell candy and refreshments at home matches and tournaments; (6) summer tournament work; (7) maintain bulletin board; (8) represent wrestling team at student and community affairs; (9) organize bus trips to away matches; (10) produce posters.

These girls are invaluable to your wrestling program. Make sure that you recognize them in a special way at your awards assemblies.

• Keep a bulletin board exclusively for wrestling in a prominent place in the school. Newspaper articles, schedules, team standings, individual records, and any other items pertaining to wrestling can be placed neatly on the board. In the off-season, you can advertise the various camps and clinics along with various wrestling pictures.

• Display a wrestling ladder in or near the wrestling room. This should list the various boys in each weight class and whom they have to defeat to move up the ladder.

• Pictures or large posters with the names of former outstanding wrestlers create interest and motivation. Hang these in the wrestling room and other prominent areas of the school.

• Become friendly with the sports editor of the school newspaper. Put him in charge of calling in meet results to the local papers. Try to encourage some of your own wrestlers to write wrestling stories for the school newspaper.

• If possible, film or video-tape all wrestling matches. These not only serve as instructional material, but can also be used as promotion techniques at assembly programs, school clubs, and parents club meetings.

• Make sure you talk with parents after meets concerning their sons—not only about wrestling but about all aspects of school life with which you might be connected. Send each parent a post-season letter.

• Arrange trips to nearby colleges for your wrestlers and Mat Maids. Keep a file on all colleges seeking wrestlers, so you might be able to help any of your wrestlers who are interested in furthering their education.

• Ask the school library to subscribe to various wrestling publications and purchase various books on the sport—and make them available to the student body.

• Try to conduct home meets in an impressive and professional manner. Make sure you have a good announcer, one who has some knowledge of the sport. Make sure that everyone can see the scoreboard and the clock. Design your programs so that they have a place for scoring, contain the rules of wrestling, and also feature a bit about each team and its outstanding performers.

• End the season with a Wrestling Dinner. To such an affair, we invite the school administration, the Board of Education, the mayor, the Mat Maids, and our Recreation Wrestling Coaches—along with anyone else the boys feel had something to do with our program.

NOTE: The coaching staff will present awards, such as Outstanding Freshman, Sophomore, Junior; Most Improved Wrestler; Most Dedicated Wrestler; Outstanding Wrestler; etc. Our principal gives an award to the boy who most exemplifies the spirit of wrestling. Finally, we announce the captains for the following year.

Part II

Pinning and Takedowns

1

Go for the Pin

by Gary L. Scott

**Former Head Wrestling Coach
New Palestine High School
New Palestine, Indiana**

As head wrestling coach at New Palestine High School, Gary Scott compiled an overall record of 45-12-1 with four sectional championships, three conference titles, and three invitational championships. He is presently head football coach at Tri (Indiana) High School.

Go for the Pin

High school wrestling is currently undergoing a significant shift in its basic philosophy, changing from a riding, holding, and stalling exercise to a faster, more dynamic form of competition.

Two factors are primarily responsible for the new emphasis. In 1971 the national rules were revised to award six points for each fall that was scored in a dual meet, as opposed to only three points for each decision won. Perhaps more importantly, officials are now encouraging increased action by frequently warning and penalizing wrestlers for lack of aggressive action.

Since the rule change clearly intends to encourage aggressive attempts to score a fall, and since falls are rewarded with double points in a dual meet, we decided to emphasize this aspect of wrestling in our program. The result has been so rewarding for our team that we plan to work even harder at pinning in the future.

We believe it has been our key to success.

APPROACH

We go for a pinning situation anytime during the match.

Some coaches and wrestlers think it is unwise to attempt to pin an opponent who is fresh, and therefore perhaps more dangerous, early in the match. Our thinking is that most wrestlers are keyed up at the start of a match and may be more likely to make a mistake that can be converted into a pinning situation. Consequently, we instruct our wrestlers to go for a pin regardless of the time elapsed in the match.

NOTE: In looking back at the results of more than 700 individual matches over the last three years, this philosophy has
not cost our wrestlers a single match, while going for the fall at
every opportunity has won many matches that otherwise might
have been lost, through the accumulation of enough "near-
fall" points to win the decision.

It is also tough to reverse a wrestler who is aggressively
going for the pin, since the bottom man has his hands full staying
off his back.

We feel that aggressive action from the top position is especially important when our wrestler is superior. The double
points scored by a pin could be the difference between winning
and losing an entire meet.

NOTE: More than once we have won meets against stronger
teams who won more individual matches, but did not score
falls. We did!

SUCCESSFUL PINNING COMBINATIONS

In keeping with our over-all coaching philosophy, we try to
stick to simple, proven combinations that the average-ability
athlete can master with enough practice. We drill on at least
some aspects of pinning at every practice session, devoting some
20-25 percent of our practice time to pinning drills.

The combinations we emphasize are the half nelson, cross-
face cradle, and near-side cradle.

Half nelson: This is still one of the most effective means of
turning an opponent onto his back, since it affords great leverage. We want our wrestlers to use the half nelson whenever they
can.

We feel the half nelson can be used whenever the bottom
man is flat on his stomach and either arm is at a 45-degree or
greater angle from his side. The half nelson is very effective in
combination with the arm bar, hammerlock, or head lever, and
we constantly look for that 45-degree angle to secure the combination.

NOTE: If the bottom man turns his head away and braces with

his opposite leg in order to counter the half nelson, he leaves himself open for the cross-face cradle.

We also teach the "force" half nelson, telling our wrestlers to apply all their weight to the forearm across their opponent's neck and then grasp that arm from under the opponent's upper arm to pry him over.

NOTE: This move seems to work particularly well in the heavier weight classes.

Perhaps the most important point in using the half nelson is the element of surprise. Shoot it quickly and drive hard, all in one motion, before the opponent has time to counter.

Cross-face cradle: This pinning hold is quite popular in our area and is used with good results at both the high school and college levels. We work hard on this maneuver throughout the year, emphasizing cradles in our practices and telling the wrestlers to look for cradles whenever they are in control.

In teaching the cradle, we want first to break the opponent down to the mat, then look for him to pull up a leg as he tries to gain his base. As soon as a leg moves upward toward the head, the top man should post the leg, with his wrist behind the bent knee and keeping his weight on the opponent's hips to prevent him from gaining a base. The top man should then quickly "cross-face" his opponent, driving the head around and down.

NOTE: This last maneuver cannot be accomplished in a lei-surely manner. All possible force should be used.

After locking the opponent's hands, the top man should walk around the feet of the cradled opponent to "shorten up" the hold.

From this position, the opponent can be brought to his back by either the "rock-back" or "roll-through" technique.

The rock-back is accomplished by lifting the opponent and turning him onto his back. It is by far the safer of the two moves, since the roll-through involves pulling the opponent across the top man's body by rolling under and lifting the cradled man.

NOTE: Although we teach both methods, only those wrestlers who demonstrate great proficiency are permitted to use the roll-through.

The wrestlers are instructed to look for a close knee-to-head relationship in any situation. Anytime the opponent's far knee is in close proximity to his head, the cross-face cradle can be applied.

This hold has been a valuable weapon, scoring points on about 90 percent of the occasions that our wrestlers have achieved a lock-up of the hands. It has scored falls on about 30 percent of the occasions it has been used.

Near-side cradle: This has also been an extremely effective hold, scoring falls a great percentage of the times that the opponent can be turned over with it. We emphasize aggressive use of the head to "lock-in" with this combination.

The opponent's head and near leg are grasped, after which the wrestler in control must drive his forehead into the opponent's lower ribs. When the bottom man bends to relieve this pressure, the arms are locked around his leg and head.

NOTE: The head should not be removed at this point, but should be used to help drive the man onto his back.

Like the cross-face cradle, the near-side cradle can be applied whenever the head and knee of the down wrestler come close together. An alert wrestler can often pop in a cradle when his opponent tries to stand up.

We try to teach our wrestlers to recognize cradle opportunities by using a five- to ten-minute drill in which the bottom wrestler moves at three-quarter speed and intentionally exposes himself to being cradled, deliberately creating close head-to-knee relationships.

The top man rides with his head up and tries to recognize and take advantage of situations as they arise. If he misses an opportunity, the bottom wrestler lets him know and returns to the position to show him. After two to three minutes, the wrestlers switch positions and resume the same drill.

NOTE: We also use arm-bar and head-lever combinations, and a few of our wrestlers have used leg-ride combinations successfully. We do not emphasize the use of leg-rides, however, because fewer pin opportunities occur with this type of wrestling.

DEFENDING AGAINST THE PIN

Just as important as scoring falls in dual meets is not losing by a fall when faced with a superior opponent. Most small high schools find it difficult to fill all 13 weight classifications with top-notch wrestlers, leaving some "soft" spots in the line-up. To be successful in dual meets, these average and below-average performers must be mentally and physically prepared to go the distance against a superior opponent—not get pinned.

The first step in defending against pinning situations is mental preparation. The wrestler must be made aware of the fact that being on his back is one of the toughest situations in any sport, and that he will have to make a supreme effort to escape being pinned.

We tell our wrestlers that they can't be pinned if they concentrate on their shoulders and simply refuse to give in, no matter how tough it gets. We also tell them that there is no acceptable excuse for being pinned, that it only happens to those who quit.

> NOTE: We further emphasize this point with a rule that everyone must remain seated when one of our wrestlers loses by a fall. No one offers consolation or helps the pinned wrestler from the mat.

Avoiding pins pays off in team points and helps establish a personal pride in never quitting. In a number of cases, we've had boys spend half a match or more on their backs and not give up.

Believing that this will power can be learned, we drill at least once a week on escaping from pinning situations. The drill lasts one-half to one minute and we use various pinning combinations. Each wrestler takes at least three turns on the bottom.

The best way to avoid pins, of course, is staying off your back. We drill on this quite often throughout the season. Starting face down on the mat, the bottom man must try to return to and maintain his base, while his opponent attempts to break him down and turn him over.

> NOTE: No escape or reversal attempts are permitted. The

bottom man must concentrate on maintaining his base and countering the pinning attempts.

The top man is also helped by this drill, since he learns to go rapidly from one hold to another in trying to turn over his opponent, closely simulating an actual situation that often occurs if the bottom man is ahead on points late in the match.

2

Pinning with the Inside Ankle Ride

by Dean Hermes

Head Wrestling Coach
Williston High School
Williston, North Dakota

Dean Hermes has been head wrestling coach at Williston High School since 1969. He is a former graduate and North Dakota State Heavyweight champion from Williston. Hermes received his B.S. and M.S. from the University of Montana, where he was a two-time runner-up in the Big Sky Conference Tournament (1963-64). He was named Coach-of-the-Year (1971) in North Dakota and has compiled a ten-year record of 76-24-2. Coach Hermes is the retiring president of the North Dakota Coaches Association and a member of the State High School Advisory Board for high school wrestling.

Pinning with the Inside Ankle Ride

As wrestling has grown, the popularity of the pin and its accompanying near-fall points has become one of the most emphasized and "coached" phases of the sport. In fact, the pin has become the most popular and familiar phase of wrestling—not only for the wrestler but for fans as well.

NOTE: Rule changes in recent years have certainly increased the importance of the pin. By making a pin worth twice as many points as a decision, the outcome of many dual meets and tournaments has been changed.

OUR PIN PROGRAM

A boy must learn to become a "pinner," and in our program we try to emphasize and encourage the wrestler to learn as many pin combinations as possible.

We begin our first practice and each practice session throughout the year with drills ending in the pin. In addition, we have an awards and recognition program for boys who have the most pins and the quickest pins in each weight class throughout the season.

NOTE: One of our state champions, Ed Maisey, now a 126-pound varsity wrestler at Brigham Young University, currently holds the North Dakota state record for most pins in a season at 27, and the most pins in a three-year varsity career at 57. Our 1975 varsity team set a new Williston High School record with 230 pins in one season.

In the past several years, we have found that as the wrestler has become more pin alert, the counters and defenses against the pin have become more effective.

INSIDE ANKLE RIDE COMBINATION

Our favorite pin has come from an inside ankle ride combination (See Photos 1, 2, and 3.) It gives us the important advantage of leg control. By attacking only the hindquarters, beginning wrestlers are not as liable to make the mistake of working too high and getting reversed or losing their top advantage.

NOTE: It is easy to learn and can be worked into at least two other pin positions—the leg pick-up and turk pin (Photos 4, 5, and 6), and the reverse cradle pin (Photos 7, 8, and 9).

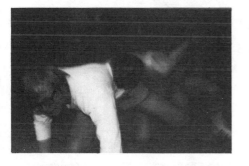

Photo 1

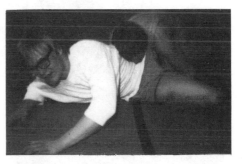

Photo 2

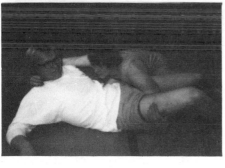

Photo 3

Photo 4

Photo 5

Photo 6

Photo 7

Photo 8

Photo 9

THREE MOVES

The inside ankle ride to crotch lift pin:

1. A grasps B's right ankle with his right hand, pulls out on B's left knee with his left hand, and pushes his head against B's left hip (Photo 1).
2. A forces B down onto his right hip by pulling on B's right leg and pushing with his head (Photo 2).
3. A takes an inside "crotch ride" with his left arm and grasps deeply around B's back with his right arm. From here A begins to lift B's leg and shoots a reverse half-nelson or cradle under B's left arm (Photo 3).

NOTE: The most opportune time to shoot the pin is when B looks back at A or when he begins his roll away from A.

OPTION

If B cannot be broken down to his right hip, A has the option of switching to the leg lift and turk pin because he is still in control of B's ankle and leg.

This technique is illustrated in Photos 4, 5, and 6:

4. A lifts B's left leg upward with both hands (Photo 4).
5. A steps over B's right leg with his left leg and drives forward encircling B's leg at the knee (Photo 5).
6. Upon driving B to the mat, A releases his hold on B's leg and overhooks or tucks B's left arm, driving his elbow towards B's ear (Photo 6).

Our next pinning option occurs if B maneuvers to stand up or reaches back to work to free his legs. Because we have good inside leg control, his position of working towards his legs enables us to easily secure the "reverse cradle" pin.

This technique is illustrated in Photos 7, 8, and 9:

7. As B maneuvers to stand up or work to free his legs, he

enables A to easily encircle B's head with his hand that was controlling B's ankle. He can now lock his hands around B's head and near leg (Photo 7).

8.   A drives into B, forcing him to his shoulder (Photo 8).

9.   When A's shoulder drops below B's, he can drive and lift B onto his back for near-fall points or a pin (Photo 9).

CONCLUSION

The "basic skill work" has now been laid for securing this pin. Getting behind, riding, and breaking an opponent down are all parts of this pin, and through our experience we find that this simple series has been very successful in developing good wrestlers plus making them pin alert.

3

The Importance of Takedowns

by Bill Garland

Head Wrestling Coach
Moorhead State College
Moorhead, Minnesota

Bill Garland's overall record as head wrestling coach at Moorhead State College is 136 wins, 78 losses, and 5 ties. In 1964, Moorhead State won the NAIA national wrestling tournament and Coach Garland received the Coach-of-the-Year award. Bill Garland has appeared at numerous wrestling clinics and was on the staff of the U.S. Olympic Wrestling Development Camp in 1965.

The Importance of Takedowns

We consider the takedown the most important offensive weapon in wrestling. Some people might feel that pinning combinations are more important; however, a wrestler must take his opponent to the mat before he can pin him.

NOTE: Another aspect to consider is that a wrestler doesn't usually pin an opponent of equal ability—and in reality, those are the ones he has to worry most about beating.

It's usually the wrestler with the greater takedown ability that wins. The wrestlers start the match on their feet and if either wrestler gets an escape, they're back on their feet—so here is the beginning of many of one's offensive moves.

Set-ups: We spend about 60% of our practice on set-ups for takedowns—feeling that the set-up for the takedown (getting one's opponent to make the move one desires) is even more important in being able to accomplish the takedown than the actual moves involved in the takedown itself (maneuvering an opponent for a single leg takedown and then completing the takedown).

NOTE: Our most difficult task is teaching the set-ups for each takedown and also making the wrestler conscious of the potential takedowns his opponent opens for him. In other words, if a wrestler is well defensed for one type of takedown, he has to be weak for another type (i.e., if he's defensed for leg tackles, he is exposed for arm drags).

Three takedowns: To be effective, a wrestler must have at least three takedowns he can do with almost equal ability. This eliminates one's opponent from defensing only one takedown.

This is especially true if they have competed against each other before—or if it becomes known that a certain wrestler can use only one takedown effectively, or uses only takedowns that originate from the neck and triceps tie-up in the standing position.

TIP: Our wrestlers have used this knowledge to their advantage as they would not tie-up with this wrestler in the standing position.

Philosophy: We feel that if we can take an opponent out of his style of wrestling on his feet, we have a much better chance of taking him down and therefore a better chance of beating him. Statistics have shown that the wrestler who gets the takedowns usually wins. We also feel that an escape (1 point) and a takedown (2 points), starting from the referee's position on the mat, are better than a reversal (2 points).

4

Coaching the Takedown

by Del Tanner

Head Wrestling Coach
Rosemead High School
Rosemead, California

In his five years as head wrestling coach at Scottsbluff (Nebraska) High School, Del Tanner's teams compiled a 41-22-1 record in dual and triangular competition. Along with the record, his teams won two district and two Big 10 conference titles. At present, Coach Tanner heads the wrestling program at Rosemead High School.

Coaching the Takedown

A boy out for wrestling doesn't shoot a good takedown the first, or the tenth, time that he tries it. The takedown, as simple and fluid as it appears, will take the "average" high school wrestler two or three years of hard work to perfect.

> OUR TAKEDOWN: Although I coach many different take-downs to my wrestlers, my favorite one is the "double knee drop heel hook." In this takedown, the wrestler drops to both knees as close to his opponent as possible and, while dropping in, extends one leg behind the opponent's leg and pushes his backward.

There are three phases of any good takedown: (1) the set-up of the opponent; (2) the takedown itself; and (3) the follow through. I feel that the most important part of the takedown is the set-up. The choice of takedown used depends upon what the coach likes and what the wrestler can do. The follow through is simple. All it consists of is making sure that a move, once started, is carried through to completion. Here is how I tell my boys to set up their opponents and some of the drills I use in my wrestling program.

SETTING UP THE OPPONENT

The proper set-up stance has the wrestler with his weight evenly balanced in the middle of his feet, neither on the balls of the feet nor the heels. If the weight is on the balls of the feet, the wrestler will have a tendency to lean too far forward. If his weight is on his heels, he is definitely off balance. Each wrestler must find his own balance point.

If the wrestler can imagine that he is a piano player assuming proper position for playing the piano, he'll fall into the best position—knees slightly bent, back straight, hips loose, elbows into body, lower arms out in front of body with palms *down*. I always emphasize that my wrestlers keep their palms down because, if they don't, their opponent will be able to slap their arms up easily and drop in under them for a takedown.

> THE CROSS-STEP: In setting up his opponent, the wrestler should take relatively small steps. I never tell my boys not to cross-step. Why? Most wrestlers are coached that the cross-step is wrong and will quickly (too quickly) move in to catch another wrestler off guard and be off balance and vulnerable themselves.

I coach the strong foot forward or "staggered stance," with the right foot (if the wrestler is right-handed) ahead of the left. This is a "sucker" stance. It encourages the opponent to charge in and take the wrestler down without regard to his own position. If the opponent goes for the wrestler's inside leg, the wrestler can flatten out on him or counter with an inside switch. If he goes outside and gets a leg, the wrestler can always rely on the whizzer or use a long arm counter.

> TRY AND TRY AGAIN: A wrestler should repeatedly try to set up and take down his opponent. One or two failures in a row mean little when they might finally have thrown the opponent off balance.

DRILLS FOR THE TAKEDOWN

Following are four drills that I use to teach my wrestlers proper takedown form and reaction. They have proven to be an important factor in our success.

• In order to emphasize the importance of keeping the hips loose, back straight and head up during the takedown, we use this drill. A wall in the wrestling room is padded and each man walks up to it as though it were his opponent. He then drops in to

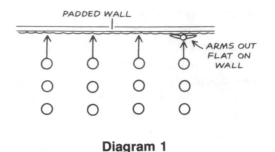

Diagram 1

the wall so that his body is touching it from his knees to his head. His arms should be outstretched as if ready to encircle the opponent. The most frequent mistake in shooting a takedown is dropping the head—this drill will cure it!

As Diagram 1 shows, there might well be four lines of wrestlers doing alternating drop-ins. It is important that each wrestler do at least 20 of them at each practice.

● During the past year, I tried this gimmick out and it worked perfectly. I attached a football *tackling* dummy to the ceiling by a rope tied on to a spring, as in Diagram 2. The spring gives the dummy plenty of "life" and makes the drill more interesting. Each wrestler approaches the dummy, drops in on his knees (head and back up with arms outstretched) and completes the move with a heel hook. We emphasize pushing the opposition over with no more force than absolutely necessary— they are told not to lift the opponent during this takedown.

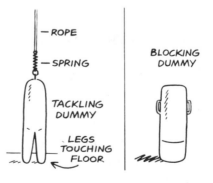

Diagram 2   **Diagram 3**

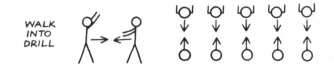

WALK INTO DRILL

Diagram 4

- Football *blocking* dummys come in several weights (Diagram 3). I use the 16 pound dummy (foam rubber) for this drill. The procedure of the drill is the same as that of the preceding drill. The only difference is that each man stretches his leg as far back as he can when he heel hooks. This repeated exercise gives the wrestler flexibility in the groin region and gets him used to extending the leg many times (a big help in stopping the slide back).

- In the drill shown in Diagram 4, two lines of men take turns walking into each other. One of the men keeps his hands over his head, while the other drops in to him and takes him down. Then they exchange roles and the first man takes the second one down. I have the boys keep their arms up so that they will not counter the man that takes them down. This gives the takedown man the feeling of live "bait."

5

Variations for the Double-Leg Takedown

by Ken Bernabe

Head Wrestling Coach
West Windsor-Plainsboro High School
Princeton Junction, New Jersey

Ken Bernabe has been head wrestling coach at West Windsor-Plainsboro High School since the school opened two years ago. The first year, wrestling a JV schedule, WWP compiled a 10-2 mark. In 1976-77, with no seniors, Coach Bernabe's grapplers went 9-4. He is now in his seventh year of coaching, with an overall record of 41-13-2.

Variations for
the Double-Leg Takedown

In considering the many different kinds of wrestling holds, and the techniques prescribed for each, one cannot but reflect on the greater importance of some of them.

We stress the teaching and execution of a considerable number of wrestling holds, but we have developed a philosophy of wrestling that places a great deal of emphasis on the takedown.

It is our basic premise that getting a takedown is the most important phase of wrestling.

We try to instill the attitude that if our wrestlers can take their opponent down, they will beat him. Beating your opponent on his feet is a vital factor in the outcome of any wrestling match.

BASIC APPROACH

We usually teach five takedowns. We concentrate on three of these five takedowns and teach a series of variations that can lead to each.

At that point, we reinforce each maneuver with intense drilling and situation wrestling, thereby trying to make each maneuver or counter automatic with each wrestler.

THE DOUBLE-LEG TAKEDOWN

The double-leg takedown is probably one of our most successful takedowns, yet its degree of difficulty is minimal.

We begin our November practices with teaching the double-leg as a basic takedown technique because it is the most familiar to wrestlers and is simple to teach.

Most important, a young wrestler can achieve a fair degree of confidence and success by using it.

Our double-leg takedown is taught from three variations. In order to effectively execute the takedown from any of the variations, there are several cardinal rules that each wrestler should follow.

CARDINAL RULES

1. Approach should be an arm's length away from your opponent. If you're too far away, you'll be vulnerable to a possible snap-down spin around, or even to a pancake by your opponent.

NOTE: We tell our wrestlers to be close enough for a tie-up, but still in good position to set up the opponent from a non-tie-up position.

2. Another paramount technique is the drop or penetration step. This is simply the exaggerated movement of either foot, enabling the wrestler to get under his opponent adequately. We drill the drop step every day for about seven to eight minutes during the first month of practice.

NOTE: We've found that proper utilization of the drop step has enabled our wrestlers to achieve better execution of both the double-leg and single log takedowns.

3. The last technique we emphasize is one that many novice wrestlers neglect—keeping the back straight (or, in more proper terminology, arching the back). By arching your back, you take away your opponent's ability to sprawl, or to shoot a cross-face or a whizzer.

"BLOOD-AND-GUTS" DRILL

I use a very simple drill to reinforce this last technique. It's called the "blood-and-guts" drill. I simply put one wrestler up and the attacking wrestler down, in a double-leg position.

On the whistle, both wrestlers react. The standing wrestler goes into a sprawl. The attacker must draw in his opponent's hips, making sure that his back is straight.

NOTE: You can add such variations as not allowing top wrestler to use his hands, or allowing him to shoot only a cross-face, a whizzer, or perhaps a pancake.

OVER-THE-SHOULDER VARIATION

We drill the double-leg takedown from three common variations. Variation #1 is the simple over-the-shoulder technique.

After drop-stepping into your opponent, your outside leg (left) should always be up, for balance. Your right knee should be down and deep between your opponent's legs.

Keeping your back straight and your right ear tight to the opponent's hip, extend your hands (making two fists) deep around your opponent's upper legs (behind the thighs is the desired position).

By using pressure and maintaining balance off your left leg, pull in your opponent's hips and dump him over your right shoulder to the mat.

The next step is where many wrestlers allow the opponent to escape, thereby nullifying the takedown.

When taking your opponent to the mat, do not let him go. Maintain control of his legs, square off your hips, and don't go off your knees.

NOTE: You can easily go into a pinning combination from this situation by using a crotch and half-nelson, or even a cradle.

LEG-TRIP VARIATION

The second variation is the leg-trip. We teach our wrestlers to use this technique when the opponent sprawls, thereby making it difficult to pull in his hips and take him over the shoulder.

Should this situation occur, you use your outside leg (the left again) to trip your opponent's right leg. In order to successfully complete this maneuver, you should pull in your opponent's hips to simplify the trip.

NOTE: By pulling in his hips, you prevent yourself from overextending or losing your balance.

Take your opponent towards his back, remembering to let go of his legs as he is falling and to immediately break your fall by putting your palms down.

By doing this, you can maintain balance and control and very possibly go into a pinning combination.

SHIFTING VARIATION

Variation #3 is shifting to a single-leg takedown after initially executing the double-leg. We use this when our opponent gets a good sprawl and is about to counter with a whizzer.

We teach our wrestlers to release one leg (the right) and clasp hands around the left leg. This then is the single-leg takedown.

NOTE: If your opponent has the whizzer, don't let him pull your right arm up his back. Always stay low on the leg.

To complete the maneuver, we have our boys sit through on their left hip, pulling the opponent past them and to the mat. From here, you bulldog or overhook his right leg, while still maintaining control by placing your right arm (the arm he whizzered) in his crotch.

This move may be difficult to teach young wrestlers, who fear going underneath their opponents. We've found that constant drilling, with emphasis on staying low on the leg, has produced a certain degree of success with many of our wrestlers.

Part III

Countering, Escapes
and Reversals

1

Countering the Leg Pick-Up

by Tom Keegan

Head Wrestling Coach
St. Mary's Central Catholic High School
Sandusky, Ohio

Tom Keegan is head wrestling coach at St. Mary's Central Catholic High School. His three-year dual record is 22-5 and includes eight tournament championships (sectionals and districts), one state championship, third place in the state, and 50 individual tournament champions.

Countering the Leg Pick-Up

The takedown is fast becoming the most important aspect of wrestling, and it is for this reason that we drill not only on offensive takedowns but on defensive takedowns as well.

NOTE: At all times during a match, a wrestler should be thinking offense. Any situation can be turned into a scoring opportunity for the boy who is aggressive enough to take advantage of it.

We take each situation and drill on the possible reactions that can be made. Because of the popularity of the single leg takedown, one of the most common situations the wrestler now encounters is where his opponent has one of his legs off the mat.

BASIC RULES

Here are the basic rules we use in countering any takedown attempt:

1. Stop your opponent's penetration with your arms, shoulders, or hips.
2. Create distance between you and your opponent—no matter how slight.
3. Keep pressure on your opponent's head. Where his head goes, he goes.
4. Counter with an offensive move.

When your opponent has your leg up, there are three possible places it can be held: In front of him (Figure 1); this is best for your opponent. In between his legs (Figure 2); both men

LEG IN FRONT

Figure 1

LEG IN BETWEEN

Figure 2

LEG OUTSIDE

Figure 3

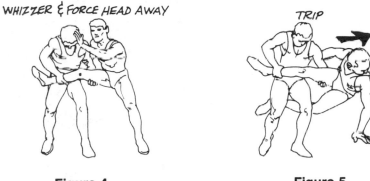

WHIZZER & FORCE HEAD AWAY

Figure 4

TRIP

Figure 5

have many opportunities from here. Outside his legs (Figure 3); this position is the best for you—try to get there. We shall now discuss the possible counters for each of these situations.

When he has your leg in front of him: Whizzer the near arm high and tight. Use your free hand to force his head down and away from you (Figure 4). Kick your free leg up so that it is perpendicular to his legs and directly behind his knees; you might want to place your free hand on the mat for balance (Figure 5). Pull your opponent backward over your leg with your whizzer arm. As you hit the mat, high-leg over the top of your opponent with your free leg. Straighten your trapped leg and work for a pinning combination.

When your leg is trapped in between your opponent's legs. Force his head to the outside of your leg with your elbow or

FORCE HEAD OUTSIDE
& SIT

Figure 6

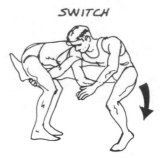

SWITCH

Figure 7

JUMP

CRADLE

ANKLE PICK

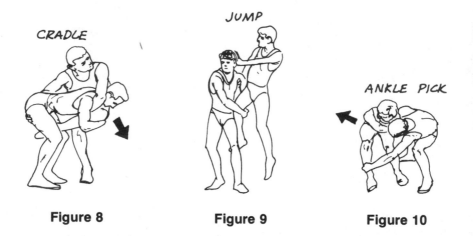

Figure 8   **Figure 9**   **Figure 10**

by taking his chin with your hand. This will remove any chance
of him using his head to apply pressure (Figure 6). When his
head is outside, use your hand or forearm to keep it down.
Now . . .

    (a) Take his thigh or buttock with your free hand and sit
hard. The force should stun your opponent momentarily. Then
either hoist your legs and go behind, or scoot your hips,
grapevine your trapped leg, and get your hips above his so that
you can go to a cross-body ride.

    (b) Take your hand off the head and drive it inside his near
thigh and fishhook the thigh. Now sit hard and switch (Figure 7).

    (c) Drive your hand over his head and under his far arm.

Grab the back of his thigh with your free hand and sit hard. When you hit the mat, scoot your hips and drive your back hand forward until you can clasp—cradle. Now hoist your legs to free your trapped leg and work the cradle (Figure 8).

When your leg is on the outside: Lock your toe behind his near knee. Whizzer his near arm high and tight. Use your free hand to force his head down and away. Now . . .

(a) Hop high into the air and pull up on the whizzer arm while you straighten the trapped leg. This should force him to let go of the leg. (Figure 9).

(b) Force him down as far as possible (if you lean forward he'll bend at the waist). Keep your free hand tight to your side and hop in a circle away from your opponent, forcing him to follow. When he steps forward with his far foot, lean down and grab it at the heel (Figure 10). Drive off your back foot to take him to the mat. When you have him down, straighten your trapped leg and work for a pinning combination.

DRILL PROGRAM

After teaching the leg-up counters, I have the wrestlers take about 10 minutes to practice them. Then I set aside six minutes (one minute in each situation for both a wrestler and his partner) of practice time to have them practice what I call the "hop drill."

Hop drill. Have man A take man B's leg in front of himself and move him around (don't take him down) for one minute. Have man B take man A's leg in front of him and repeat. Go through the same procedure with the leg in between the man's legs and also with the leg on the outside.

This drill will get both men accustomed to the situations connected with having a leg up. After the boys become accustomed to the drill, you can change it by allowing the boys to either take the man down or execute the counters. The drill should be done every night or every other night for the first week or two and occasionally for the rest of the season.

2

The Cross-Face Cradle

by Donald Rogers

**Head Wrestling Coach
Wirt High School
Gary, Indiana**

Donald Rogers, a graduate of Indiana State University, is head wrestling coach at Wirt High School. His five-year dual-meet record is 29-26. He has produced 20 conference champions and three state finalists in that time.

The Cross-Face Cradle

Have you ever picked up a book of wrestling moves and noted a move that you thought would work well for your team? If you have, and you are a new coach like myself, I'd guess that you would want to try the move yourself before introducing it to your team.

NOTE: You would probably find a partner, review the book's explanation, try the move, and soon find that you are not in the position of advantage pictured in the book. I usually attribute this to the fact that my assistant on the move either did not read the book, or did not understand his role as the loser.

If you think about this, very few opponents are likely to have read the same book, and even fewer are going to be willing to assume the loser's role. I usually find myself or my assistant asking, "Yeah, but what if," and then working on variations of the move. (This gives my assistant time to read up on his role.)

THREE BASIC POSITIONS

Through some disastrous coaching experiences, but excellent learning experiences, and some notes from an excellent coach, Bob Bubb of Clarion (Pa.) State, I will show what I have found to be the most common "Yeah, but what if's" of the "cross-face cradle."

NOTE: I will cover three basic positions: (1) The opponent broken down; (2) the opponent in the referee's position; (3) the cradle locked up and taken over. In all photos and text, the wrestlers will be identified as wrestler T (top wrestler) and wrestler B (bottom wrestler).

Break-down position: Since the cross-face cradle is best executed from the break-down position, we'll look at moves from this position first. If wrestler B moves his far arm out to prevent wrestler T from hooking the cross-face hand, several moves are possible. But in staying with cradles, wrestler T should drop back and put in a near leg cradle (Photos 1 and 2).

If wrestler T can hook the cross-face hand, but wrestler B keeps his body rigid preventing the hook-up of the cradle, wrestler T should wait for an opening under wrestler B and with his free hand reach through and grab above his cross-face hand (Photo 3). Pulling with both hands and driving across the body of wrestler B should drive him to his back (Photo 4). If wrestler T can lock up the cross-face, but cannot get it over, the knee placed in the back and used as a brace often loosens the determination of wrestler B (Photo 5).

Photo 1

Photo 2

Photo 3

Photo 4

Photo 5

Photo 6

Photo 7

Photo 8

Photo 9

Photo 10

Referee's position: From the referee's position, a wrestler can very effectively use the cross-face cradle if he has confidence in the move and is willing to move out in front to get the drive necessary to lock up the cradle (Photo 6). Often as wrestler T moves out in front, wrestler B will hook the front leg as a counter

Photo 11

Photo 12

Photo 13

Photo 14

(Photo 7). Wrestler T should continue the move, driving the shoulder to the knee and locking up the cradle.

If wrestler B tries an inside leg stand-up, again wrestler T should move to the side and put in a near leg cradle. If wrestler B does a sit-out, wrestler T should drive forward applying pressure to wrestler B's back and finish the cross-face as the knee is close to the cross-face arm in the sit-out position (Photo 8). If wrestler T cannot lock up the cradle and wrestler B starts up, wrestler T should under-hook wrestler B's free arm, step out in front, lift, and take B back and over (Photos 9, 10, and 11).

Lock-up and take-over: Unfortunately, locking up and taking over a cross-face cradle does not necessarily mean a sure pin. There is a very obstinate inside shoulder that all too often does not end up on the mat. Here are several suggestions to help solve this problem. In Photo 12, wrestler T is not whispering "Put your shoulder down" in the ear of wrestler B, but rather puts his head in a position to look into wrestler B's ear and then drives his forehead into the side of wrestler B's skull (Photo 12).

The other two methods deal with the ability of wrestler T to hook or not hook wrestler B's free leg. If the leg can be hooked, wrestler T should walk his toe back, applying pressure to the leg to help turn wrestler B's hips and shoulders (Photo 13). If the free leg cannot be hooked, then the use of the knee in the side again helps to rotate wrestler B's hip up and shoulders down (Photo 14).

3

Helping the Unskilled Wrestler Escape

by Al Wolf

Head Wrestling Coach
Conneaut Lake High School
Conneaut Lake, Pennsylvania

Alan Wolf has been coaching wrestling for twelve years and has never had a losing season. As head wrestling coach at Conneaut Lake High School, he has a three-year record of 29-10 which includes three league championships and a regional championship. While working for the State Department, Alan Wolf coached wrestling in Japan and Germany.

Helping the
Unskilled Wrestler Escape

The oldest "saw" in wrestling is for a coach to ask a nationally known wrestling figure—"What must a good wrestler have?"

The answer will be equally as old as the question—"A wrestler must have balance, strength and speed."

NOTE: This is all very enlightening, but what in effect the nationally known wrestling figure is saying is—"Coach, your boy has to have talent."

That talent is needed for the champion is understood—but what about Joe Average Coach who has to field a team of twelve wrestlers, ten of whom need agility drills before they can tie their shoes?

The situation: All coaches are aware that poor wrestlers never seem able to escape, but most coaches seem unwilling to face the facts as to why. They rely on magic holds and a belief that super-speed can be taught even though the boy was born slow. What do many coaches say as they watch their untalented boy being ground into a permanent part of the mat? Generally their remarks from the bench go something like this: "Move you clod—move faster—oh no! You're going on your back—no! no!"

NOTE: After a few years of experience and an acceptance that fate does not deal man a perfect hand every time, that the cards must be played as they are—the coach will yell: "Get up, any way you can; just get out from under there."

Natural abilities: In short, the coach comes to depend upon a boy's natural abilities. In the first instance above, the coach has probably recognized that his boy has little strength—but he failed to recognize that he has no balance or speed either. The boy is unskillfull and the middle of an important match is hardly the time to be practicing. In the second instance, the coach has realized the boy's shortcomings and is keeping these shortcomings from being exploited—as the boy is working hard to maintain his balance thereby utilizing the ability he has. As we shall see, the first boy doesn't have a chance but the second boy just might win.

A look at escapes: Let's take a close look at escapes. All escapes have the same flaw in common which keeps the untalented from getting out, but which doesn't bother the talented as they can skillfully maneuver beyond this flaw.

In order to move at all from the bottom a wrestler must lift one knee or the other which automatically tilts his hips and throws him off balance. To make matters even worse, the wrestler at this stage, whether it be a sit-out, a stand-up, or a switch, is balanced only on one leg. Only amazing dexterity can get him past this point and to the next. The man on top merely pushes or pulls and down goes the bottom man.

EXPERIMENT: As an experiment, lift your outside knee as if you were going to do a sit-out. Have somebody pull your outside hip at that time. Down you go. With a poor wrestler—there he stays.

This is the same on an outside leg stand-up or a switch. The talented wrestler is not plagued at this point because he has the agility to regain his balance by either getting both feet under him or by sitting firmly on his buttocks where it will take tremendous force to dislodge him.

NOTE: Even if the maneuver is blocked, the agile wrestler can easily chain wrestle to another; however, the poor wrestler is ground into the mat with no possibility of executing any portion of the chain.

Natural balance: How can the poor wrestler be taught to get out if his opening move will cause him so much trouble? He can learn how to utilize his natural balance during this initial move by not moving too rapidly. This should be self-explanatory—but somehow wrestling coaches as a group insist that speed can win over all other courses of action. This is a fallacy because nobody can do anything successful at a speed beyond his skill.

Try any motor action which requires skill, such as golfing or baseball. Hit the ball smoothly. Now double your speed and watch the comic-farce. The skilled wrestler can move reasonably fast from the bottom because of his increased skill—but the unskilled will fall flat.

The unskilled wrestler on the bottom must therefore be able to lift his knee and hold his balance at the same time while moving through the maneuver to reach his buttocks or feet never faster than his agility will permit.

> **TIP:** If the hold begins with an outside knee lift, it's difficult for the poor wrestler to keep from being gut-wrenched. If the hold begins with an inside knee lift, the poor wrestler must make sure that all his weight is leaning away from the inside knee— or else the good wrestler will pull him onto the inside knee, forcing the outside knee up, and down he goes.

Outside vs. inside knee: While raising the outside knee, the poor wrestler must concentrate on getting the inside arm free thereby giving him a chance. This lessens the effectiveness of the gut-wrench. The outside knee is probably a superior move in producing wrestlers because of the greater options from it—such as switch, sit-out and stand-up, while the inside limits most wrestlers to just a stand-up.

However, if your area is a gut-wrench area, the inside knee is probably the only way your poorer wrestlers can escape. Again, it must be pointed out that the wrestler must sag away from the gut-wrench and struggle to his feet, holding his balance.

If your area is an ankle-grabbing one, the poor wrestler will do better raising the outside knee and holding his balance while completing the maneuver. Again, stress balance and the need to reach both feet or both buttocks—otherwise the ankle-grabber will tilt the boy on one leg or one hip and down he goes.

General tips: The good wrestler can get mighty excited when the novice just plain refuses to fall over. The skilled wrestler can do some awfully stupid things against somebody who stubbornly refuses to roll over and play dead, and who keeps chugging away at a basic hold.

Conditioning can now be a factor—and agility dies with an out-of-shape boy. This could prove to be the equalizer or the clincher in the final period; thus, keep your poor wrestler moving steadily, but with balance.

With balance the score doesn't get out of hand—and most of all your poor wrestler doesn't get pinned. A 3-0 match score doesn't make a hopeless situation during the last period. Even if the boy loses against a top-flight wrestler, his ego hasn't been smashed—therefore, watch him go next week against an average wrestler.

Wrestling drills: Here are some drills especially effective for the unskilled wrestler:

1. On whistle have top man use any set first move—such as ankle-grab, gut-wrench, chin-hook, etc. Then after a one-second delay have the bottom man move smoothly and powerfully to both buttocks or his feet. Bottom man must not permit himself to be driven to mat.

2. On whistle have bottom man practice freeing an inside arm or either ankle before initiating his first move, then proceed to base.

3. Have bottom wrestler lift outside knee and balance on that foot and inside arm. Top wrestler now tries to drive bottom man to the deck—but bottom man must gain balance on both buttocks or his feet.

NOTE: This we call the "balancing act" drill—and it's a difficult but effective one.

4. Bottom man leans hips away from top wrestler, partially raising inside knee; as top man pulls bottom wrestler toward him, bottom pulls away and gets inside foot on mat until force of top man pulls bottom man on inside foot and to his feet.

5. All and any agility drills are most helpful—particularly those in which bottom man starts on hands and knees (sit-out, turn-over, etc.).

4

Combination Moves for Escapes and Reversals

by Steven A. Weiss

**Head Wrestling Coach
Fenton High School
Bensenville, Illinois**

Steven A. Weiss wrestled in high school and college before turning to coaching the sport. At Niles East High School (Skokie, Illinois), he placed second in the state tournament. He then went to Northern Illinois University on a wrestling scholarship and was undefeated in conference and dual meets. At present he is head wrestling coach at Fenton High School, with an overall record of 119-43, which includes four conference championships, two district championships, and one sectional and one state championship.

Combination Moves
for Escapes and Reversals

Many high school wrestlers when attempting to escape from the bottom position make one move and then stop. This gives the offensive wrestler enough time to counter and secure control of the bottom man.

NOTE: From the underneath position, we emphasize combination moves or escapes that combine two or more different maneuvers in rapid succession. In this way, our wrestlers learn the value of mobility and how to escape after their initial moves are countered.

This article will present various combination moves which can be utilized from the referee's position as escapes or reversals.

CRAWL-OUT AND SWITCH

One effective combination move is the crawl-out and switch. Wrestler A in the dark jersey moves as fast as he can on his hands and knees while wrestler B in the light jersey attempts to follow.

When A feels B hanging on his legs, he quickly turns to the side to switch. Wrestler A has the option of switching B to the inside or outside. In some cases, the bottom man will escape on just the crawl-out if he moves hard and fast. See Series A —Photos 1, 2, and 3.

SIT-OUT

There are three combination moves that can be worked

Photo 1 (Series A)

Photo 2 (Series A)

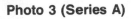

Photo 3 (Series A)

from the sit-out. In Series B, wrestler A makes his first move a sit-out. As wrestler B follows, A hooks his wrist, turns in, and executes a side roll. See Series B—Photos 1, 2, and 3.

Photo 1 (Series B)

Photo 2 (Series B)

Photo 3 (Series B)

Photo 1 (Series C)

Photo 1 (Series D)

Photo 2 (Series D)

The sit-out switch combination is another option that may be used. Wrestler A "sits out," and as B follows he "swings" a power switch to either side. See Series C—Photo 1.

Another combination move from the sit-out is the stand-up. See Series D—Photos 1 and 2. Wrestler A starts his stand-up after sitting out in front of B. To make his stand-up effective, A moves back into B by pushing backwards off his heels from the sitting position. At the same time, A works on B's hands to free himself.

STANDING SWITCH

The stand-up has become a popular escape not only in college, but in high school wrestling as well. There are two excellent stand-up combination moves that can be employed. The first is the standing switch. See Series E—Photos 1, 2, and 3.

Wrestler A is up to his feet and wrestler B is right behind him with his hands locked around A's waist. Wrestler A fakes a switch to one side by swinging his arms and hips and then switches B to the other side.

NOTE: Once the wrestlers go down to the mat, wrestler B may not lock hands and therefore A is given more freedom to execute his switch.

Photo 1 (Series E)

Photo 2 (Series E)

Photo 3 (Series E)

Photo 2 (Series F)

Photo 1 (Series F)

Photo 3 (Series F)

STANDING SIDE-ROLL

Another combination maneuver from the stand-up is the standing side-roll. Wrestler A sets up B for the side-roll by starting to work on B's hands. He then grabs hold of one wrist and turns his body to the inside so that he is almost perpendicular to B.

NOTE: In executing his side-roll, wrestler A drops to his elbow and flips B over to his back with a lifting movement from his knees. See Series F—Photos 1, 2, and 3.

SWITCH SIDE-ROLL

The switch side-roll becomes an effective combination move when the initial switch attempt is blocked. See Series G—Photos 1, 2, and 3.

Photo 1 (Series G)

Photo 2 (Series G)

Photo 3 (Series G)

Wrestler B is shown blocking A's attempt to switch by driving into him. Wrestler A begins his side-roll by hooking B's wrist that is around his waist. At this position, he quickly turns inside so that his body is perpendicular to B's body and completes his roll.

CONCLUSION

When teaching combination moves, the coach should stress the importance of moving fast with two moves in mind in case the first one is countered.

Generally speaking, the wrestler who stops moving when countered and only tries one type of escape, is usually the wrestler who loses.

5

Basic Escapes
from the Underneath Position

by R. G. Macias

Head Wrestling Coach
Mankato State College
Mankato, Minnesota

Rometo "Rummy" Macias' 14-year dual-meet record at Mankato State College is 232-118-9. His wrestling teams have won the Northern Intercollegiate Conference 13 years out of a possible 14. Add to that two NAIA team titles and ten NCAA University place winners.

Basic Escapes
from the Underneath Position

It's my contention that wrestling can be taught on all levels by stressing a few basic movements from various positions. From there, a beginner can build his repertoire, and with work and experience become a polished wrestler.

Taking into consideration individual differences, I stress basic movements which fit the majority of the group. To illustrate the point, here are four basic movements used in escaping from the underneath position.

1. SIDE ROLL

(a)   Grasp opponent's wrist with outside hand.

(b)   Bring outside knee to inside knee.

(c)   Bring top inside foot to opponent's inside thigh.

(d)   Rotate opponent over back, *hanging onto wrist.*

(e)   Drill the man with your inside shoulder.

(f)   Get at right angles.

(g)   Shift the hips toward opponent's feet. This will cause the left foot to be where the right was and vice versa.

(h)   Make your turn at right angles, dropping your inside arm between you and your opponent. This is where you finally *release the wrist.*

HELPFUL HINTS: (1) Push into opponent and crowd him—the

less daylight the better. (2) Keep the outside shoulder high and drop to the elbow rather than the shoulder—you get more pull. (3) Rotate the body rather than pull. (4) Stay in a ball and bring nose to inside knee.

Counters: (1) Step over planting leg toward your head. (2) Re-roll, squeezing inside knee of opponent with both of your knees, help regain knee position by staying parallel and pulling with arm around waist. (3) Keep weight back. (4) Elbow push and toe hook behind knee, stay parallel.

2. SIT OUT

(a) Place outside foot 6" forward and 6" to the side.

(b) Slide out directly in line with top man hitting inside hip like a baseball slide.

(c) Make the slide on your elbow and inside hip.

(d) Bring trailing knee into your stomach and continue turn.

(e) Pull away—throw pivot arm up to block opponent from coming around.

HELPFUL HINTS: (1) Sit out directly in front of top man—a straight line from the bottom man to direction of sit out. (2) Release the knuckles around the waist before sitting out—daylight is needed. (3) Bull your neck as you complete your sit out. (4) Bringing trailing knee into the stomach allows weight to be shifted to lower part of body a split second sooner—thus freeing your arms for attacking or countering.

Counters: (1) Short way, check the pivot arm above and behind the elbow so opponent can't pull it back. (2) Reach for the rear end—place chest on his back—spin and allow him to carry you around with his turn, fall off toward his feet staying on your knees. (3) Don't go over the inside arm. (4) Long way, when opponent has done a good sit out and is facing you, you can go opposite way.

3. SHORT SWITCH

(a)   Push down from hands raising knees about 3 inches, allowing inside leg to pivot outward.

(b)   Shift inside leg away from opponent landing on *outside* hip on mat at approximately where outside knee was.

(c)   Cup the outside hand and reach for own hip pocket.

(d)   Slip cupped hand inside opponent's near thigh.

(e)   Straighten arm and body and crawl away on heels at right angles *breaking opponent's shoulders to mat.*

(f)   With other hand grab near end and jam opponent forward as you complete reversal.

HELPFUL HINTS: (1) Knock the opponent's arm off your elbow before starting swtich. (2) Emphasize top man's shoulder to mat instead of pivoting. (3) Leverage must be gotten from opponent's thigh only.

Counters: (1) Straighten inside leg that is being hooked. (2) Pull arm so it's hooked below elbow—step over with both legs and end up at right angles. (3) Shoulder crowd—lower inside shoulder end and crowd with inside hip, hit near arm inward. (4) Pull arm that is being switched. (5) Re-switch.

4. STAND UP

Outside Leg:

(a)   Release knuckles around waist with outside hand.

(b)   Plant outside foot at previous spot of outside hand.

(c)   Push back against resistance, standing firmly on both feet.

Inside Leg:

(a)   Move outside knee inward (center of body).

(b)   Release knuckles around waist with outside hand.

(c)   Plant inside foot at previous spot of inside hand.

(d)   Push back against resistance, standing firmly on both feet.

HELPFUL HINTS: (1) Resistance must be released around waist before an attempt to stand up is made. (2) Pushing back must be made directly against resistance, not to the right or left, otherwise balance is lost. (3) Bend at waist and knees when attempting to stand. (4) Force inside arm inward, turn arm around opponent's thumb. (5) Keep feet apart.

Counters: (1) Start of stand up: Trip opponent's inside leg with outside leg forward, keep a deep waist and force inward, hack inside arm inward, make first move when your hip hits the mat. (2) Half stand up: Drop down and pick up opponent's nearest ankle with both hands, pick up high and go through leg pick-up series trip. (3) Three-quarter stand up: Hook opponent's inside leg from behind with your inside leg, slide arm to opponent's small of back, keep head in front position of opponent, cup opponent's far inside thigh, plant outside leg in front of opponent, force opponent toward his back using side of head and outside leg as leverage.

Part IV

Practice Sessions

1

The Practice Room: Where Wrestlers Are Made

by Howard "Buck" Anderson

**Head Wrestling Coach
Napoleon High School
Napoleon, North Dakota**

In his six years as head wrestling coach at Napoleon High School, Howard "Buck" Anderson has compiled a truly enviable record. His grapplers' accomplishments include: a 66-13 record in dual meets, five straight regional championships, one regional runner-up finish, two state runner-up finishes, and the North Dakota State Championship in 1975. Coach Anderson has received two Coach-of-the-Year awards.

The Practice Room:
Where Wrestlers Are Made

The practice room is the place where good wrestlers are made. Great wrestlers are often naturals, but they can only become great through good practice and exposure to excellent competition.

Each part of practice must have a reason behind it. The wrestler should understand how each drill or activity is improving him as a wrestler or helping him get into superb condition.

Our practices never last more than one and a half hours, with about 40 minutes of activity the night before a match.

This is probably shorter than most practices, but if one keeps active the wrestler will learn a great deal in a short time and get into condition faster.

The chance of injury is also greatly reduced. A broken thumb is the only injury that has kept one of my wrestlers out of competition in six years.

THREE BASIC AREAS

Our practices are divided into three basic areas:

1. A period of *exercise and stretching* (15 to 20 minutes).
2. A period of *learning* a particular move or group of moves (one hour).

NOTE: In this period, we start out slowly and end up wrestling full speed on each move.

3. A period of *conditioning* (10 minutes).

PRACTICE OUTLINE

Below is an outline of an average practice, with the reasoning or psychology I use for teaching these moves. This is not complete, but the outline has worked for us.

Make the changes you want to and see if it is an orderly way to cover what you want to teach. Changing what is covered each night adds variety.

NOTE: "Fun-and-Gut Drills" will also add interest. Some of these are listed after the daily practice schedule.

I certainly hope this is something you coaches can tack up on the office wall and use.

I. EXERCISE AND STRETCHING

ACTIVITY: *Running*. Three to five minutes of running steps or laps in the gym. Never more than 5 minutes—running in wrestling shoes is hard on the feet.

REASONING: Running works all muscle groups and tends to take away stiffness. The aim is to break a sweat.

ACTIVITY: *Short Calisthenics*. Ten repetitions. Exercises include jumping jacks, toe touches or windmills, burpees, fingertip push-ups, sit-ups, leg raises, chain breakers, bridges, hurdler's exercise, groin exercise. Also do a pin drill, such as cradles, arm bars, etc.

NOTE: A spin drill may occur simultaneously.

REASONING: Calisthenics strengthen all muscle groups. Later in the season, we often skip all calisthenics to get in more wrestling and to break up the daily routine.

NOTE: If wrestlers don't know what's coming next they are attentive and cooperative.

Hurdler's exercise, bridging, and groin exercises are aimed at avoiding injury to the neck, groin, and knee areas. This is also a time to talk about the week's schedule, ranking, and other areas of interest.

II. LEARNING

Below are most of the moves used in this part of practice. We start out passive for short periods of time and progress to 1-minute periods of full-speed wrestling.

ACTIVITY: *Set-Ups and Takedowns.* These require quickness and aggressiveness, both of which are difficult to teach but come with confidence and experience.

NOTE: Half of all practices is spent on set-ups and takedowns.

REASONING: If we can take someone down, we can beat him. If we can ride the opponent, we can dominate him. From the bottom, we want to work our opponent with the least amount of energy expended.

1. Set-ups: Drop step. Draw step. Circle and come back. Hand fighting. Single arm ties. Arm drags, cross arm, near arm. Russian ties.

REASONING: Set-ups are more important than takedowns themselves. If you don't know where to start on a takedown, you don't know a takedown.

2. Takedowns: Single leg/double leg. Fireman's carry/head lock. Shrugs/duck-unders. Muscle moves—bear hugs, wranglers, and lateral drop; head locks and arm-under series.

REASONING: The first three are low-risk takedowns, but highly effective. By low risk, we mean a takedown where your chances of success are high and your opponent's chances are poor.

Muscle moves are high-risk moves, but effective. We use them when we are behind by up to 5 points, or against a weaker opponent.

ACTIVITY: *Riding.*

REASONING: Be able to ride when you have to. If you can't ride an opponent, let him go. A pin hold is the best way to ride anyone. A cradle is almost like legal locking of the hands. Never ride anyone just to hang on—it's too much work.

1. First move on top: Deep waist, far ankle. Deep waist, near ankle. Blast (which is far tricep, near leg, and drive over). Crunch (which is arm-over hook, deep waist, knee in crotch). Cross-face, far ankle. Iowa ride.

REASONING: Sometimes we start with group-one rides on wrestler in referee's position and move from there to show the rider that they work.

2. Ride loose and counter: Hook (which is deep waist and underhooking an arm).

REASONING: Some wrestlers react well to any situation, and for them it's better to keep their heads up, hips in, and to ride loose.

To hold on to the opponent, we use the under-hook on the arm and the deep waist, alternating the under-hooked arm and deep waist as the bottom man turns. The bottom man does most of the work.

3. Leg riding: Cross-body ride. Jacob's ride. Figure 4. Grapevine.

REASONING: We work with some wrestlers individually on leg riding after it has been introduced to all wrestlers. We feel the best leg riders are those who can also ride using most methods other than leg riding.

ACTIVITY: *Reversals and Bottom Moves.*

1. Ride counters and bottom moves: Peeling hands. Maintaining balance. Staying on all fours.

REASONING: Be able to counter every ride your opponent uses.

NOTE: We work as much on ride counters as we do on reversals.

Make a move; wait for the counter; work on the counter; and move when the opening is there for the escape or the reversal.

Never try a reversal until you have broken your opponent's ride.

2. *Reversals:* Stand-up (inside-outside leg). Sit-in (rather than sit-out). Switch (inside and outside).

REASONING: These are used as first moves and the start of other chain moves.

III. CONDITIONING

ACTIVITY: *Conditioning Exercises.* Wall jumps. Chopping in place, hit the mat on all fours, stand up on whistle. Quick calisthenics for five to 10 minutes. "Big four" on Universal Weight Machine—incline sit-ups, stomach flexor, pull-ups, dips.

REASONING: This is the toughest part of practice. Everyone feels good when it's over. It builds confidence and strength.

"FUN-AND-GUT" DRILLS TO BREAK MONOTONY

1. *Tag-team wrestling:* 2-on-1 or 2-on-2.

2. *Reaction drill:* Two wrestlers lie side-by-side. On the whistle, they react fast to try to get top position.

3. *Cage ball:* Divide the team in half and roll out the cage ball. The wrestlers fight to force the ball to the opponent's end of the mat.

4. *Fighting the pin:* Put a larger opponent on top of a wrestler, with a pin hold on him. The wrestlers go until the bottom man gets off his back.

NOTE: In this drill, the top man is usually one weight class heavier than the bottom man.

5. *Fighting cross-face:* On the whistle, grab your opponent's legs. Staying off your belly, fight the cross-face. Basically, just hang on to the leg until the whistle blows again.

6. *Work-up:* Start with one wrestler flat on his belly, another on top of him. Blow the whistle. The bottom man works to his knees, then to his feet, and stops.

2

Organizing Wrestling Practice

by Edwin M. Johnson

Head Wrestling Coach
Jefferson High School
Daly City, California

Edwin M. Johnson has led his Jefferson High School wrestling team to a three-year record of 56 wins and 4 losses, including a league championship in 1972. In addition to coaching the wrestling team, he serves as the school's athletic director.

Organizing Wrestling Practice

I'll attempt to give coaches who are faced with the problem of small or inadequate facilities some useful ideas on the better use of time and what facilities they do have.

One of the essential items in the development of any wrestling team is adequate mat space. Adequate mat space allows a maximum number of wrestlers to do what is most important in their personal development—actual wrestling.

NOTE: When a coach is bound by lack of either space or mats—or both—he must organize his practice sessions with these restrictions in mind.

I was one coach who found himself with less than outstanding facilities: one mat and one small room with unpadded walls. After much experimentation, I now use the "circuit theory" as the basis for our practice sessions.

WHY USE THE CIRCUIT THEORY?

The circuit theory is probably used to some extent in almost all well-organized wrestling programs, but in ours it is the basic structure of all our practices.

With our facilities, we cannot possibly have more than 12 wrestlers working safely at any one time. Although we can place more than 12 on the mats in warm-ups and controlled skill-learning periods, it is not in the best interest of the athlete to overcrowd the mats during wrestling drills and competitive situations. Our team roster of 60 complicates the problem.

The circuit theory gives each athlete as much mat time as

possible, and gets maximum use out of the available mat space, by rotating the athletes among various workout stations. In that way, everyone can be kept busy without overcrowding the mat, and there won't be a long line of wrestlers waiting for a chance to get on the mat.

ELEMENTS OF THE WORKOUT

The daily workout schedule is concerned with the three basic elements of any sport: activity, conditioning, and strength.

Activity, in this case wrestling, is the single most important item in the workout, consisting of skill development, situation wrestling, and competitive wrestling.

Conditioning deals with the athlete's cardio-vascular development and includes distance running, sprints, and endurance wrestling.

Strength is aimed at development of the large muscles, which is best brought about by the "overload" principle, weight training, and isometric exercises.

PLANNING THE WORKOUT

In planning practice organization, you must determine your priorities—those areas you feel must be developed to get your wrestlers ready, not only for league and dual-meet competition, but also for league tournaments, sectionals, and, perhaps, state competition.

Much of our planning is determined by the pre-season conditioning and strength aspects of our program, and our notes on how closely the athletes are following pre-season workout schedules help to determine the early phases of the seasonal practice schedule.

NOTE: We encourage increased work on conditioning and strength early in the fall semester, but it is really a year-round activity.

The degree of conditioning and strength and the skill-level of our returning veterans, will also help set the stage for early practice.

THE WORKOUT

Chart I is an example of a typical practice session with a time limit of approximately two and one-half hours. Many variations of this schedule are used during the season and it can be altered according to the needs of the team or the individual concerns of the wrestlers.

NOTE: We believe new wrestlers can learn from watching, as well as competing with, experienced wrestlers, so we make an effort to give our varsity competitors the toughest competition available.

2:45 — Team meeting.

2:50 — Explain goals of session; break up into Groups A, B, and C according to weight class:
Group A — 95 to 120 lbs., lightweights
Group B — 127 to 145 lbs., middleweights
Group C — 154 lbs. and up, heavyweights

2:55 — A 45-minute session; each group rotates every 15 minutes to the next station until all groups have been at all stations; the stations are set up in the wrestling room, weight room, field, and parking lot. The starting set-up is:
Group A — Warm-up, skill drills, situation wrestling.
Group B — Distance running, exercises.
Group C — Weight training, exercises.

3:45 — A 45-minute session; rotation every 15 minutes.
Group A — Skill development (mat room).
Group B — Rope climb, flexibility exercise.
Group C — Sprints.

4:30 — A 30-minute session; groups rotate every 5 minutes for 2 repetitions.
Group A — Situations, competitive wrestling.
Group B — Stretching exercises and run.
Group C — Isometrics and partner drills.

5:00 — Special drills, team meetings, conditioning, warm-down.

Chart I

The coach should be creative in his approach to the workouts. Tape recorders and development games can be used to make the practices run smoothly and provide variations that make them enjoyable, as well as helping to achieve the goals set for maximum team development.

SUGGESTIONS FOR BETTER WORKOUTS

One helpful aid in using the circuit theory of practice organization and team development is the preparation of a wrestling handbook to explain the procedures and outline workout schedules. Other helpful contents include pre-season conditioning ideas, workout areas, wrestling clinics, lists of AAU wrestling meets, and wrestling camp information. The coach should distribute the handbook in mid-Spring and take time for a team meeting to answer questions and explain the theory to his wrestlers.

SOME PROBLEMS

Repetition by the coaches is one of the problems created by the circuit theory. Sometimes coaches have to repeat a presentation as many as four times, depending on the number and type of stations used.

This can lead to boredom and loss of interest on the part of the head coach or his assistants. In my experience, however, I have found it as much a learning process for me as a problem. It allows me to evaluate the various methods and approaches I use, and, I hope, to do a better job of presenting my material. This is one of the reasons why good assistant coaches are invaluable in creating effective practice sessions and workouts.

Good team leaders of the various groups are also essential, since it is of primary importance that the athletes be willing to complete the circuit as prescribed by the coach. If the athletes do not accept the need to complete the entire circuit and do all the required work, then all the planning and presentations by the coaches are wasted.

NOTE: Some of the more highly skilled athletes will probably have to spend additional time working with each other after the regular practice sessions have been completed, but this is not necessarily a problem. In our case, they are and have been very receptive to this need. In any case, it will depend on how hard they work and how much they accomplish during each session.

CONCLUSION

I am sold on the circuit theory as a way to organize wrestling workouts. Not only has it been successful, but it places a great deal of responsibility on the individual athletes—a very positive thing to learn from any athletic program. At the same time, it allows them to get extensive wrestling experience despite limited facilities.

Also of note, the circuit theory approach, by making the utmost use of our facilities, has allowed us to continue a "no-cut" policy in our program. That is, it has allowed any boy to become a member of our team, so long as he meets the minimal demand that he be at every practice both mentally and physically.

Just remember—it is essential that the coach be sold on his approach to practice organization. Use your creative abilities and enjoy the results—your athletes may gain a new insight into the once dreary chore of practice.

3

Use Every Minute
of Your Wrestling Practices

by Mike Story

Head Wrestling Coach
Belton-Honea Path High School
Belton-Honea Path, South Carolina

Mike Story came to Belton-Honea Path High School in 1970 as an assistant in wrestling, football, and track. He became head wrestling coach in 1971. Since Coach Story came to B-HP, the wrestling teams have a 58-6 meet record with four regional titles in six years.

Use Every Minute
of Your Wrestling Practices

Wrestling requires much from its participants, not only in terms of physical exertion, but also in self-discipline and self-sacrifice.

It is our belief that we must use every minute of practice time to maximum efficiency if we are to totally prepare the wrestlers.

We use periods of instruction that allow the wrestlers to recuperate, so they can get the most out of periods of exertion. Even during our periods of drill instruction, resistance is used to allow the wrestlers to get a true feel of the holds they are working on.

FIRST WEEK PRACTICE

We begin our first week of practice with explanations of team rules and regulations and of what wrestling is all about. We make clear what will be expected of all our candidates in the weeks to come and emphasize the need for hard work and dedication, as well as getting into and staying in shape.

First workouts involve running, jumping rope, and familiarizing wrestlers with the positions and stances they will be using on the mat, as well as the drills we will be using in the early going.

We also include explanations and demonstrations of illegal and potentially dangerous holds.

NOTE: We feel this is an important part of early instruction, so that bad habits don't have a chance to form. If these holds are shown early, wrestlers can be careful with their use in practice and avoid costly injuries.

I am a firm believer in starting the wrestlers down on the mat early in the year to allow them to learn to fall and roll correctly. This gives them more confidence when they start wrestling from a standing position.

Here is a sample schedule we might follow for the first few days of the season. After the first day, explanation of stances and illegal holds would be replaced by periods of instruction and conditioning.

FIRST DAY SCHEDULE

3:15 to 3:30

Meet with candidates and explain team rules and what is expected of them. Outline the objectives of the sport and what they can expect from you.

3:30 to 3:40

Warm-ups, including: (1) side-straddle hop, (2) stretch between the legs, (3) trunk rotation, (4) push-ups, done slowly in sets of 10, (5) sit-ups, bent-knee type on 4-count, (6) sit-ups, abdominal-twisting type on 2-count, (7) neck bridges, front and back.

3:40 to 3:45

Run the "train" for ½ mile, alternating sprint and jog.

3:45 to 3:55

Introduce wrestlers to referee's position and get each wrestler into both the top and bottom positions to find what seems comfortable to them.

3:55 to 4:05

Introduce wrestlers to standing position, stressing importance of developing a good stance. Again, we try to let wrestlers be as comfortable as possible. Let them get the feel of moving side to side and forward and back, without losing their stance or crossing their feet.

4:05 to 4:15

First demonstrate illegal holds, making sure the wrestlers understand the penalties for using them. Then show potentially dangerous holds and emphasize that the man using the hold is responsible for his opponent's safety.

4:15 to 4:20

Have two of last year's wrestlers perform a short exhibition match to demonstrate match procedures, how points are awarded and why. Stop the match at intervals to fully explain what has gone on and points awarded.

4:20 to 4:30

Introduce the basic drills that the wrestlers will be using during the early part of the year. For us, these are:

1. Spin drill: This teaches wrestlers to work for position behind the opponent and teaches the defensive man to prevent this from happening.

> NOTE: Down man cannot use hands, but can use lateral movement in defensing the spin. Up man can use hands to try to get position.

2. Ride the horse: Teaches the wrestler to maintain good position behind his opponent as the defensive man moves quickly around the mat trying to escape. Done in rounds of 30 seconds each.

3. Drop step: Drills the fundamentals of penetrating on leg takedowns. We usually do at least 100 of these per day, in addition to other work we may do on takedowns.

4:30 to 4:40

Let the wrestlers pair up (by size) and wrestle down on the

mat. This is to acquaint each athlete with the feel of the mat and to get him familiar with wrestling positions and match procedure. Lasts about two minutes each.

4:40 to 4:50

Run the wall. Space wrestlers along the wall, leaning on wall with outstretched arms, and have them run in place. Three minutes. We vary the pace and emphasize high knee lift. Then pair up wrestlers and have them jump rope 300 times.

After a day or two of this indoctrination, we begin our more concentrated type of practice.

SAMPLE PRACTICE SCHEDULE

3:15 to 3:25

Warm-up period led by team captains. We use the same basic exercise group we used the first day, but increase speed and repetitions.

NOTE: We emphasize sharpness and execution from the very beginning, to remove any tendency toward being sloppy or lackadaisical.

3:25 to 3:55

Takedown drills: (1) drop steps, at least 100, (2) single-leg and at least one counter, (3) double-leg and at least one counter, (4) fireman's carry and at least one counter.

3:55 to 4:20

Takedown wrestling. Wrestlers pair up for 30-second takedowns. Each pair must go eight times, with each boy getting as many takedowns as possible in 30 seconds. Unless a pin is imminent, they get right up and start again after each takedown.

4:20 to 4:45

Reversal and escape drills: (1) outside switch and at least one counter, (2) inside switch and at least one counter, (3) stand-up and at least one counter.

4:45 to 5:15

Breakdown and pin drills: (1) tight waist series and counters, (2) head lever series and counters, (3) crossface series and counters, (4) nelson series and counters, (5) cradle series and counters.

5:15 to 6:00

Wrestle down on mat: (1) one-minute sprint round, (2) three-minute round, (3) 30-second sprint.

NOTE: This period may be lengthened considerably as a conditioner in the early going or over the holidays.

6:00 to 6:10

Run the wall and continuous movement. Once the wrestlers are spaced along the wall, they are called onto the mat in groups of four. While those on the wall run, those on the mat chain-wrestle for 30 seconds. Each man must move at maximum speed. The four on the mat return to the wall during a jog interval and four more take their place.

NOTE: This can be repeated and the intervals varied as needed.

6:10

Make announcements and pack it in.

COACHING OBJECTIVES

Through our practices, we try to give each boy a selection of holds he feels comfortable using and has confidence in.

Next we try to expose the wrestler to as many on-the-mat situations as possible. We try to arrange for each of our wrestlers to face opponents in practice who use varied styles of wrestling and have different body types.

We also work hard to get the wrestler in the best possible condition.

Our wrestlers must have the endurance to chain-wrestle (move continuously) the entire last period, if necessary.

PRE-TOURNAMENT PRACTICE

When we are preparing for post-season tournaments, we usually modify our regular schedule, since we need to handle fewer and more experienced wrestlers. We try to stress technique, and keep just enough conditioning work to keep the edge on them.

NOTE: Chart I illustrates a typical pre-tournament practice.

We have found that this type of end-of-season practice allows the wrestler to maintain his endurance, and also allows him to recover from a long season and any minor hurts he may have.

```
3:15 to 3:25 —  Warm-ups
3:25 to 3:45 —  Takedown drills
3:45 to 4:00 —  Takedown wrestling
4:00 to 4:20 —  Escape & reversal drills
4:20 to 4:40 —  Breakdown & pin drills
4:40 to 5:00 —  Wrestle down on mat
                (1) 30-sec. sprint
                (2) 2-min round
                (3) 30-sec. sprint
                (4) 2-min. round
5:00 to 5:05    Run wall & continuous
                movement
5:05          — Make announcements;
                go in
```

Chart I: Pre-Tournament Practice

CONCLUSION

We have found that it's necessary to spend quite a bit of time early in the season on developing skills. This usually entails extensive use of drills and situation wrestling.

NOTE: We usually teach new moves "by the numbers" and build speed as the steps of the move are mastered.

This period of drill work serves to (a) get our wrestlers off to a sound start, with good habits, and (b) allow our more experienced wrestlers to brush up on skills and expand their repertoire.

As the season progresses, we spend less time on drills and more on situation wrestling. We also use the approach of teaching a counter to a move as soon as we teach the move.

NOTE: We feel it is imperative that our wrestlers learn as many counters as possible.

Whenever possible, we let the drills carry through from the initial move to the fall. We find this increases offensive skills, in addition to individual aggressiveness.

If a wrestler is taught from the beginning to work for the pin from all situations, the attacking style of wrestling that we favor is quickly developed.

4

Using Stations for Better Practice Organization

by Gerald S. Bandola

Head Wrestling Coach
Cedar Ridge High School
Matawan, New Jersey

Gerald S. Bandola has been head wrestling coach at Cedar Ridge High School ever since the school was founded eight years ago. In those eight years, Coach Bandola has established Cedar Ridge as a perennial wrestling powerhouse, compiling a 100-21-1 record in dual meets, which includes seven district championships and 47 individual champions.

Using Stations for
Better Practice Organization

Most coaches are probably confronted with the problem of not having enough time for drilling, conditioning, and getting things done in general.

It seems that every time you come up with a way to work on conditioning, you lose time for drilling. Or you have a couple of wrestlers working on the mat, while the rest just sit around doing nothing because of poor organization or lack of mat space.

When we began our program eight years ago, we were confronted with the same problem. But through experimentation, good planning, and some imagination, we came up with a solution.

We feel that we've conquered this problem by employing stations in our practices, allowing us to accomplish many things in less time.

FOUR ADVANTAGES

First, all the wrestlers are working. No one sits around the wrestling room for any length of time.

Second, we can wrestle, drill, and work on conditioning all at the same time, with no apparent waste of time.

Third, we've been able to cut down on our practice time. This is good because the wrestlers can no longer dog it in practice, and they realize that shorter practices allow them more time to pursue outside interests.

Fourth, it affords us an opportunity to utilize our varsity wrestlers as teachers. This frees the coaches to work with boys individually or to supervise a particular aspect of a drill.

USING YOUR BOYS AS TEACHERS

As coaches, most of you will probably agree that your kids are your best teachers.

An example of this would be when a member of last year's team returns to practice and teaches one of your current team members a new move.

The next day your wrestler will probably say, "Hey, coach, look at the new move Joe taught me," and you'll shake your head in disgust because it's the same move you tried to teach him earlier in the season.

Working on the principle that a boy will try harder to learn from a fellow wrestler he looks up to and respects, we have our junior varsity wrestlers drill with the varsity men in the same weight class.

In our school it's traditional that a graduating senior is responsible for producing a horse to replace him. This has become a great pride factor with our kids.

GENERAL SET-UP

In organizing the stations, we utilize either three or four stations, depending on what we want to do at that particular practice or portion of practice.

Before going further, however, let me explain a little about our situation to give you an idea of how we adapted this system to our wrestling room.

In our auxiliary gym, we have a 38 by 38 foot wrestling mat, which is bordered by 12 feet of free space between it and the walls.

We like to set up our stations in the following manner (see Diagram 1):

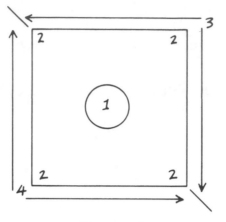

Diagram 1

Station I: The center of the mat.
Station II: The four corners of the mat.
Station III: The free space around two adjacent sides of the mat.
Station IV: The free space around the other two sides of the mat.

NOTE: Stations III and IV are located on the bare concrete floor. If you have any spare mats, these areas should also be covered.

A typical drill cycle lasts 12 to 16 minutes before the wrestlers have an opportunity to sit down and rest, or before they start the whole cycle over again. The duration is determined by the coach.

NOTE: The duration and intensity of the drill cycle depend on the time of the season and whether the coach wants the boys to work hard on a given day.

Let's say that on a particular day we want to concentrate on takedowns. We would probably use the following drill cycle.

TAKEDOWN DRILL CYCLE

First, we divide the squad into five or more groups of eight wrestlers, grouped according to weight (see Chart I), with the

Group A – 101, 108, 115, 123 lbs., Varsity and JV
Group B – 129, 135, 141, 148 lbs.   "   "   "
Group C – 158, 170, 188 lbs., hwt.   "   "   "
Group D)   Group E) – Remaining wrestlers pair up

Chart I

varsity wrestler being paired with the junior varsity wrestler in each weight class.

NOTE: If your squad is very large, you can form a sixth group.

All wrestlers in Group A start at Station I, where they wrestle live takedowns for 1 minute with their weight-class partners.

At the end of 1 minute, the varsity wrestlers rotate to the next J.V. wrestler for another minute of live takedowns. (See Diagram 2.) This procedure continues until the varsity wrestler returns to his original man.

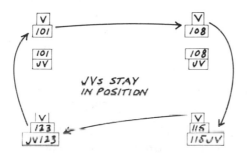

Diagram 2

At the end of four minutes, Group A moves to Station II. Group B moves to Station I and goes through live takedowns in the same manner.

At Station II, Group A drills on takedowns for the next four minutes. The coach should have the wrestlers drill on takedowns or portions of takedowns that would necessitate use of the mat (ankle picks, the finish for single or double leg takedowns, etc.).

NOTE: Group A at Station II starts on the same whistle as Group B at Station I, and does not stop drilling until it is time to move to the next station.

At the end of four minutes, Group C takes over at Station I to wrestle live takedowns; Group B moves to Station II to drill on takedowns; and Group A moves to Station III.

At Station III, the wrestlers practice set-ups for takedowns. (For example, drills on stance, hand control, set-ups for the different takedowns.)

At this station, the wrestlers again drill for four minutes, starting and stopping at the same time as the boys at Stations I and II.

NOTE: At Station III, the coach must make certain the wrestlers do not become overzealous, since they are working off the mat and could easily be injured on the floor.

Station IV could consist of conditioning for another four minutes, if the coach feels a need for it. Or the coach could cut the time to a certain number of repetitions of exercises.

Here the coach could have his wrestlers perform 25 pushups, 50 situps, 10 pullups, or any other exercise he wishes, and then let them rest until the next cycle begins.

The activity at Station IV depends entirely on the philosophy and imagination of the coach toward calisthenics or the drilling of particular moves.

Chart II shows a few examples of how the stations can be used to cover different aspects of wrestling.

As you can see, the number and variety of things that can be done are limited only by the coach's own creativity and imagination.

CONCLUSION

I would like to say at this point that we never wrestle for more than four minutes in any given drill cycle during practice, yet our wrestlers seem well-conditioned in the third period of a bout or the final rounds of a tournament.

Stand-Ups	Offense	Defense
Station I	Live	Live
Station II	Hand Control	Ankle Traps
Station III	25 Reps., Alone	Counter Hand Control
Station IV	Conditioning	Conditioning

Pinning Combinations		
Station I	Live	Live
Station II	Armbars	Counter Armbars
Station III	Cradles (¼ Speed)	Counter Cradles
Station IV	Conditioning	Conditioning and Bridging

Chart II

You should also take into consideration the fact that we do not have a recreation or elementary school program, so we have to try to accomplish as many things as possible in the shortest possible practice time if we are to compete on an equal footing with other schools that possess more extensive programs.

In closing, I would like to add that I only hope the utilization of stations is as beneficial to your program as it has been to ours.

5

Situation Scrimmages for High School Wrestlers

by Hubert N. Wagner

**Head Wrestling Coach
Middlebury Union High School
Middlebury, Vermont**

Hubert N. Wagner has been head wrestling coach at Middlebury Union High School since the sport was introduced there seven years ago. His dual-meet record is 106-33-4, which includes four state championships. Wagner holds three Coach-of-the-Year awards.

Situation Scrimmages
for High School Wrestlers

Wrestling has been an interscholastic sport at Middlebury Union (Vermont) High School for only seven years. This, combined with no program in the junior high school, has resulted in our first-year wrestlers being completely inexperienced. This inexperience not only includes lack of skill knowledge, but lack of "mat sense" in strategic situations.

> NOTE: Our problem is to provide the wrestlers with experience in the tactical situations they will face in interscholastic matches. We divide these situations into two groups—the strategic (involving point differences) and the technical (involving various rides, etc.). Here's how we teach both.

STRATEGIC SITUATIONS

In the strategic situations, we assign points to each wrestler and set a time limit. The following are some of our strategic situations:

1. Neutral position, 30 seconds remaining in the match, one wrestler ahead by 1 point, and no time advantage. The main objective in this drill is to teach the wrestler to go all out when behind and wrestle aggressively but intelligently when in the lead. Care must be taken that stalling is not permitted.

2. Wrestler in control leading by 2 points, and 30 seconds left in the match. The man in control must wrestle aggressively, but he should be aware that he should give up the escape if he gets in trouble rather than be reversed.

3. Wrestler in control has his opponent in a pinning combination with 30 seconds left in the match, and has completed the requirements of a near fall, thus giving him a 1-point lead.

The objective here is to teach the wrestler in control to maintain his balance and keep his opponent on his back. If he must allow anything, he should allow his opponent to turn to his stomach and escape the pinning combination—but not score any points.

4. One wrestler in control with the score tied and 30 seconds left in the match. Both wrestlers must go all out to gain the win. The top man must wrestle aggressively, working for the pin or predicament or near fall points, yet he cannot allow the defensive man to score or he will probably lose. The bottom man must realize that when he wrestles more aggressively, the top man must counter his moves and has less chance to work a pinning combination. He knows that he must escape or reverse to win.

NOTE: In these strategic situations, the wrestlers will exchange positions, and usually each man will be in each situation twice.

TECHNICAL SITUATIONS

In the technical situations, we scrimmage on the basic moves that are practical in certain situations. We feel that by scrimmaging in specific situations, the wrestler will automatically react and move with confidence when he is confronted with them.

1. Tight waist and ankle ride: This is a very popular ride in our area, and it can cause problems for the wrestler who is not prepared to attack it. We scrimmage for a 30-second period, with the top man working for the pin and the bottom man working for an escape.

Basically, we want our bottom wrestlers to post the controlled ankle with the knee pointing to the ceiling, pick the hand off the ankle, control it, and then move immediately while he has control of the hand.

2. Cross body ride: While we feel that not all our wrestlers will become skilled at leg wrestling, each man should be able to counter leg rides.

Here, while the top man is working for the guillotine, split-scissors, or Jacobs' pin, we want the bottom man to sit toward the grapevined leg and come up in control with the cross body ride. If this is not possible, he should control his opponent's left arm (assuming the grapevine is with the first leg) with both hands and sit towards the grapevine, extending the opponent's arm under his body and laying back to flatten out his opponent—and then come up on top.

3. The whizzer: When drilling in this situation, we use two positions. First, the wrestlers are in a neutral position such as a counter for a takedown, and, secondly, the man applying the whizzer is in the down position.

From this series, we teach a variety of moves. For instance, we teach the man applying the whizzer the bump-and-pull to break down his opponent, and the man being whizzered is taught the limp arm—as the first moves in the series.

Other moves for the man being whizzered which we have found effective are the "head chancery" if his opponent turns his head toward him, and the "roll through" if his opponent has a strong bump-and-pull. He must time the bump and the roll when the opponent bumps, or he can get caught on his back.

NOTE: The man applying the whizzer can bump and then spin away from the bump to a neutral position, scoring 1 point if he was in the down position.

4. Neutral position with man on his knees: In this neutral position, man A is on his knees in the double-leg tackle position and his arms are around the other wrestler's legs, but hands are not locked. Man B is standing with his arms at his sides. When the whistle blows, wrestler A attempts to secure a takedown with a double-leg tackle and wrestler B attempts to sprawl and cross-face to counter the takedown.

We let the wrestlers scrimmage until one wrestler has secured a takedown. This allows the wrestler a chance to gain confidence in his ability to use another move when the first attempt is countered. Also, the other wrestler will develop a better knowledge of countering takedowns. We hope to instill the feeling that if he can counter a takedown attempt from this situation, he should not get taken down in an actual match.

5. *Switch position with wrestler on both knees:* Wrestler A is in a switch position with wrestler B on both knees and one hand on the mat. On the whistle, wrestler A attempts to execute the switch, while wrestler B will attempt to counter the switch with either a step-over, limp arm, or re-switch. We usually place each man in each position two to four times during a practice.

NOTE: These drills are an important part of our practice sessions. We spend more time in the early season drilling on the basic moves in a non-scrimmage setting first, and then utilize them in situation scrimmages. As the season progresses, we spend less time in situation scrimmages.

CONCLUSION

These, of course, are not the only situations we use during the course of the season. If we find a certain area needs improvement, we isolate that situation and drill on it. We feel that we can increase the experience level of wrestlers more rapidly by exposing them to and drilling them in situations that will commonly occur in actual wrestling matches.

Part V

Conditioning and Training

1

Some Thoughts on Conditioning Wrestlers

by Robert A. Keller, Jr.

Head Wrestling Coach
Loyola High School
Towson, Maryland

Robert A. Keller, Jr. is head wrestling coach at Towson High School. His record there is 14 wins against 6 losses and includes two league championships.

Some Thoughts
on Conditioning Wrestlers

I believe that proper conditioning is one of the most important aspects in developing competitive wrestlers. And this proper conditioning does not simply mean training for muscular strength or the ability to wrestle hard for six or eight minutes.

NOTE: Proper conditioning is far more inclusive, in that it must allow for the development of muscular range, sharpening of muscle tone, and the building up of endurance qualities.

These items have to be built into your wrestling program since they don't just happen. They don't just happen for the athlete either—even if they are in your program. He has to have the proper attitude in approaching the conditioning in order to benefit most by it.

Here are some of the ways we have approached these problems and tried to "build in" good conditioning techniques in our wrestling program.

PRIDE IN CONDITIONING

Our wrestling program begins about three weeks before the football season ends. Many of our wrestlers are football players, but for those who are not we have a rigorous program of physical activity. It consists of a great deal of running—distance as well as sprints. The practice on the mat is of an introductory nature or a review of basics for the experienced boys, but the entire three weeks is devoted to conditioning the non-football players.

NOTE: To help instill pride in conditioning, we tell the non-football players how badly they are going to make the football players look when they finally report for practice. These boys seem to like this idea of getting into shape and being able to challenge the football players when they arrive for practice on the first day. This is a positive type of competition and one in which both groups thrive.

One of the side issues here is an old wives' tale to the effect that football conditions boys for wrestling and wrestling conditions boys for spring sports, etc. This is definitely not true. It depends on the sport because each of the seasonal sports requires different abilities.

NOTE: It doesn't hurt to play other sports per se. However if a boy needs muscular development, he has to do some of this out-of-season. He can't expect to do all of it via other sports—but only through a concentrated program.

We keep our boys appraised of what they will be doing. We also have them do more each day . . . more each week . . . than they did before. They take great pride in this and feel that it sets them apart as special.

BUILDING CONDITIONING

Once the wrestlers are in reasonably good condition, we work on an alternating system of hard days and light days to allow their bodies to respond to the pressure and build resistance.

WARM-UP: The warm-up activities are quite important before practice. We spend about 20 minutes in muscle-stretching exercises to raise the body temperature and get the blood coursing through the veins. This warm-up period, long though it is, has been a significant factor in the lack of injuries to our boys.

During practice, we work in three groups, usually designated by weight divisions. While one group is on the mat, the other two are either jumping rope or working with the weights. Both of these activities help sharpen tone and build endurance.

WEIGHT TRAINING

Some authorities discourage weight training during the season; that is, lifting weights for bulk. We agree with this but there is a great advantage in using weights for another purpose. Muscle tone can be sharpened and muscle range can be expanded by using the weights and the same exercises (military press, etc.), with the only difference being that the weight lifted be just 25% of what the wrestler can normally do. The wrestler should do about three sets of ten repetitions as fast as he can, without losing any of the technique in the exercise.

OTHER METHODS

There are still wrestlers who must develop strength and they must do it to survive the season honorably. So we employ other methods of developing strength in-season. For instance, we do a series of after-practice exercises when the day is officially over on the mat. These exercises include: push-ups with a man on your back; bridging (back) with a man on; half-squats with a man on your shoulders; from one knee, lift man off the mat; etc.

NOTE: You can use others, of course, or make up exercises. The number used depends on the type of practice held.

Pride in workouts after practice also develops to the point where the entire momentum will be taken over by the wrestlers and they will vie with one another and former records. An example of this would be sprints. We run a series of running-in-place drills, alternating jogging and sprinting. We build up on the time from week to week and once in a while throw in a challenge to the team. They really push themselves to accomplish the new goals.

SALT: When you work boys extremely hard, remember that they lose a great deal of body fluid. Thus, there is a need for salt tablets. This is a regulation with us after practice every day. Fatigue has, in general, disappeared.

DEVELOPING PROPER ATTITUDES

We do two things along this line. First, we duplicate all articles that we can on the conditioning of athletes and include them in a handbook which is then distributed to the boys. Articles on vitamins, diets, and other pertinent health information, as well as articles written by well-known athletes and coaches are included.

Secondly, we conduct a clinic for all athletes at the school covering training, conditioning, and mental attitudes for interscholastic competition. Guest speakers as well as staff members speak and give demonstrations.

FOR MORE INFORMATION

My chief source of information on conditioning has been our two swimming coaches. Coaches of swimming are vitally concerned about diet, vitamins, and the principles of conditioning and training in general. Also, check the journals on swimming for more information on these matters. The makers of the "Universal Gym" also have developed a number of ideas about training and conditioning that you might find helpful.

2

A Complete Pre-Practice Wrestling Exercise System

by Lewis W. Jenkins

Director of Athletics
Surrattsville High School
Clinton, Maryland

Lewis W. Jenkins has been coaching high school wrestling since 1966. His record at Burroughs (Maryland) Junior High School was 13-1. At his present post at Surrattsville High School, his overall wrestling mark is 93-26-2, and includes six league titles, two county championships, one district championship, and two state championships. He is also athletic director and head baseball coach at Surrattsville.

A Complete Pre-Practice
Wrestling Exercise System

At Surrattsville (Clinton, Maryland) High School, conditioning is a part of every wrestling practice session. After Christmas, we revert to what we call our 12-station pre-practice conditioning. There are 12 stations plus a warm-up station. See Chart I.

NOTE: While there are a number of variations that can be applied to this type of conditioning, we do it the following way—a sort of free-style workout.

THE PROGRAM

As soon as the wrestlers are dressed and ready for practice, they go directly to the warm-up exercises on their own. When they finish at the warm-up station, they get in groups of two or four and start at any one of the 12 stations.

NOTE: A manager will time the entire squad for 30 seconds, one minute, or two minutes, depending upon the coach's desire. Each wrestler will know this, as he is required to read the practice plan for the day before he dresses. Each time the manager blows the whistle, each group will move clockwise around the room until they have completed each station.

When the wrestlers have completed the cycle, they go to the back of the wrestling room to practice wrestling skills (not to wrestle) until the entire squad is finished. While the wrestlers are exercising, the head coach and assistant coach walk around the room to make sure that the exercises are performed correctly.

WARM-UP EXERCISES IN THE FRONT OF WRESTLING ROOM	
ISOMETRIC #3	STRETCHING EXERCISES
ISOMETRIC #2	NECK MUSCLE EXERCISES
ISOMETRIC #1	BACK MUSCLE EXERCISES
COORDINATION AND WEIGHTS	CHEST, ARM AND SHOULDER EXERCISES
MEDICINE BALL (ARM, BACK, SHOULDER, LEG AND ABDOMINAL MUSCLES)	LEG MUSCLE EXERCISES
ROPE SKIPPING-LEGS AND WIND ENDURANCE	ABDOMINAL MUSCLE EXERCISES

Chart I

TIME LIMIT: A time limit is set on the stations, not on the exercises. The wrestlers must do as many exercises at each station as they possibly can—but they do not have to follow any particular order or number of repetitions. When the whistle blows everyone moves to the next station, regardless of where he is at that particular time.

We have found this type of conditioning interesting, competitive, and enjoyable to our wrestlers. Here's the program in detail.

THE VARIOUS STATIONS

The pre-practice wrestling exercise program consists of the following stations:

WARM-UP EXERCISES

1. Jumping jacks
2. Neck rotation
3. Bicycle kick
4. Belly-whoppers
5. Running in place

Station #1: STRETCHING EXERCISES

1. Bend and reach
2. Hurdler stretch
3. Elbow touch

Station #2: NECK MUSCLE EXERCISES

1. 8-count neck exercise
2. Back bridge
3. Front bridge

Station #3: BACK MUSCLE EXERCISES

1. 4-count toe touches
2. Alternate toe touching
3. Wing stretches
4. Rocker stretch
5. Bird nest
6. Duel back stretch
7. Chinese back stretch

Station #4: CHEST, ARM, AND SHOULDER EXERCISES

1. Push-ups
2. Burpees

3. Reverse push-ups
4. Arm circles

Station #5: LEG MUSCLE EXERCISES

1. Mountain climbing
2. Bottoms up (also called crabs)
3. Russian kick
4. Squat jumps

Station #6: ABDOMINAL MUSCLE EXERCISES

1. Rowing exercise
2. 4-count sit-up
3. Leg lifts
4. Snap-ups (also called V-ups)

*Station #7: ROPE SKIPPING—LEGS AND WIND ENDUR-
ANCE*

1. Front
2. Back
3. Cross

*Station #8: MEDICINE BALL (ARM, BACK, SHOULDER,
LEG, AND ABDOMINAL MUSCLES)*

1. Two-hand chest pass
2. Back toss
3. Sit-up

Station #9: COORDINATION AND WEIGHTS

1. High jump
2. Up jump
3. Quarter eagles
4. Arm press
5. Wrist curl

Station #10: ISOMETRIC #1

1. Push-ups
2. Wrist break
3. Arm contraction
4. Trunk contraction

Station #11: ISOMETRIC #2

1. Isometric neck
2. Bridge out of pinning combination
3. Neck hold

Station #12: ISOMETRIC #3

1. Isometric sit-up
2. Leg curl
3. Leg raise

3

Interval Exercise for Wrestlers

by Gary E. Frey

**Head Wrestling Coach
Moses Lake High School
Moses Lake, Washington**

Gary "Hub" Frey is head wrestling coach at Moses Lake High School. His dual record is 93-5-2, and he has coached teams to two state and three district championships. His teams have also produced 12 individual state and 23 individual district champion wrestlers.

Interval Exercise for Wrestlers

Although good condition is an integral part of any successful athletic program, superb condition is a "must" for a successful wrestler. Most wrestling coaches, however, don't have the time to follow a program that would really bring their boys to "peak." This is not true of Moses Lake's interval exercise program. It puts our boys in top condition—a six-minute match becomes a "breeze." And since it only takes 25 minutes daily, it allows plenty of time for drills and teaching. Here is how we arrange our schedule.

We have 7 groups of exercises. The first group is for warming up and consists of 4 exercises while all other groups consist of 2. Each group is designed so that the athlete uses different muscles for the exercises in it. For example, if the first exercise in a group was push-ups, the next would be sit-ups or some other exercise that wouldn't require use of arm muscles.

> OVERLOADING PRINCIPLE: By alternating muscle areas within the same group, we can get the boy to exercise more than if he had to do all of one exercise and then all of the other—it seems easier to do 10 sets of 10 push-ups when each set is spaced from the next by 10 sit-ups than it does to do 20 push-ups without a break.

We never change the exercises or the sequence of the program. All we do is pile more on as the boys get tougher. The following is our set and repetition schedule for the entire season. (Figure 1.) The first number in parentheses shows the number of repetitions and the second indicates how many sets of the exercise must be done for each week of the season.

1st and 2nd week (10 x 2)	3rd week (20 x 1)	10 sprints—4 min. jog
4th and 5th week (15 x 2)	6th week (25 x 1)	15 sprints—6 min. jog
7th and 8th week (20 x 2)	9th week (30 x 1)	20 sprints—9 min. jog
10th and 11th week (25 x 2)	12th week (35 x 1)	10 sprints—6 min. jog
13th week (30 x 2)	14th week (40 x 1)	10 sprints same as above

(Sprints are length of gym; quick start to center, then taper off to a trot.)

Figure 1

BORING? It might seem that since we don't change our exercises, that the boys would get tired of the program. This is not true. We carry it out at such a fast pace that no one has time to get bored. We save time by not changing the exercises because it is then unnecessary to teach new ones. And because the exercises are the same, the boys soon learn them by heart and need little instruction in them.

Here are the groups and the exercises that we use. The first group of 4 warm-up exercises is fixed and the repetitions remain the same all season. Starting with Group II, exercise 1 (spot running) the alternating system comes in. For example, the boys would spot run for 10 seconds (more according to the chart in Figure 1 as the season progresses) and then would drop down to fingertip push-up position for 10 repetitions. They would then alternate between spot runs and push ups for the listed number of sets.

Group I

1. Trunk twisters: Standing position, arms out at shoulder level. Swing arms, while twisting body, to the left on "two." Return to start on "three." Repeat to right side ("four"). Do 10 on 4 count.

2. Windmills: Standing position, arms out at shoulder level on "one." On "two," swing right arm down and touch left foot. Return to start ("three"). Swing left arm to right foot on "four." Do 10 on 4 count.

183

3. Four count bob (right): Standing position, hands on hips, legs crossed to start. Do 10 on 4 count. (Figure 2.)

4. Four count bob (left): Same as "right" except that left leg is over right to start and counts "two," "three" and "four" are left. Do 10.

Group II

1. Spot run: Run in place for 10 seconds, drop down from running position into block position. (Figure 3.)

From block drop into:

2. Fingertip push-ups: Same as normal push-up except that it is done on the fingertips of both hands.

Alternate between 1 and 2 for 5 cycles.

Figure 2   **Figure 3**

Group III

1. One arm push-ups: Take sitting position with only contact at hands and heels. Roll to the right and do 10 push-ups. Roll to the left and do 10 more on 2 count.

2. Nutcrackers: Sitting position, left leg extended, right foot over left knee. Alternate legs on a 4 count 5 times as in Figure 4.

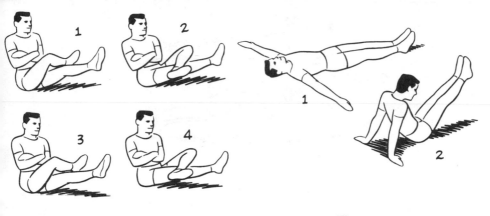

| Figure 4 | Figure 5 |

Group IV

1. *Back push-ups:* Lay on back and push up with hands behind head. Do on 2 count.

2. *Feet together-feet apart:* Lay on back with hands behind neck. Raise feet 6 inches off the mat and spread them apart slowly. Bring them back together and repeat cycle 10 times on 2 count.

Group V

1. *V-ups:* Lay on back. Do 10 on 2 count. (Figure 5.)

2. *Sitting feet together-feet apart:* Sitting position with legs extended in front and arms supporting behind body. Raise hips off the mat on fingertips and slide feet apart. Return to starting position. Do 10 on 2 count.

Group VI

1. *Sit-ups:* Standard sit-up position with arms behind neck and *knees up.* Do 10 on 2 count.

2. *Military press push-ups:* Do 10 on 2 count as in Figure 6.

Group VII

1. *Spread push-ups ("dips"):* Do 10 on 4 count. (Figure 7.)

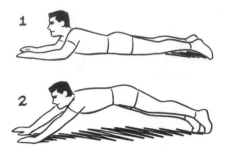

Figure 6

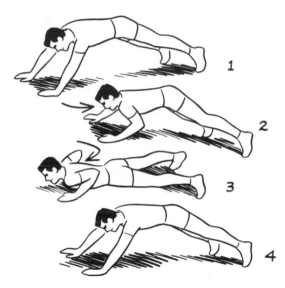

Figure 7

2. Bridging: Rock forward, backward and sideways for 2 minutes.

NOTE: Exercises 1 and 2 in Group VII are considered individual exercises. The boys advance on these at their own speed and they do not follow the weekly schedule.

4

Getting the Most Out of Wrestling Calisthenics

by Bob Cossarek

Head Wrestling Coach
Dominguez High School
Compton, California

Bob Cossarek is head wrestling coach at Dominguez High School. He began the wrestling program there and his league wrestling record is 20 wins against 6 losses.

Getting the Most Out
of Wrestling Calisthenics

One of the biggest problems in conducting a wrestling practice is giving everyone enough of a workout. This is especially true when you have a large squad in a limited area. Few will disagree that the best conditioning for a wrestler is an actual full-speed wrestling match. But when you end up with about 50 boys (after cutting the squad), you don't have the time or space to allow actual wrestling for each and every boy.

> OUR OBJECTIVE: With this in mind, we designed our calisthenics to serve not only as a warm-up for the individual—but also as a test to weed out the weaker boys and the ones not willing to give the effort necessary to become a proficient wrestler.

Our wrestling calisthenics are divided into five general areas: (1) stretching exercise; (2) one-man exercises; (3) two-man isometrics; (4) two-man exercises; and (5) running. If we limit the running to 1 mile, all of our calisthenics can be completed in about 30 minutes—and it's time well spent.

Before practice: As each boy enters the wrestling room, he will strip down, weigh himself and enter his weight on a master wall chart. At the end of each practice, each wrestler repeats the same procedure. The weight chart becomes a valuable gauge to judge such things as—the severeness of a workout, whether a boy is following a proper diet, whether he is working as hard as he should, or whether a boy may be losing too much weight.

Practice then begins with calisthenics. The team lines up

facing the coach or captain in order of their respective weights. The first man in each column is varsity, the second is junior varsity, and so on down to the last man in each division. This is also a simple way for the coach to take roll.

> NOTE: We have a wall ladder board laid out in the same manner. If there are any changes in weights or position, the coach can change the wall board before or after practice and the wrestlers will take their positions as the board dictates.

Stretching exercise: Our first exercise is always stretching. It helps us start off with the right mental attitude, if we can get rid of the aches and stiffness that generally accompany the high school wrestler before entering into vigorous exercises.

> EXECUTION: We begin by placing the hands on the hips and rotating the neck. We continue down the body, stretching or rotating each major part of the body until we finish up with the ankles. All this can be completed in about 2 minutes.

One-man exercises: The side *straddle hop* follows our stretching drills. We do 100 at quick time each regular practice. We then begin the *push-up*. We start the season with 20 and add 1 a day until we reach 40. Next, the wrestlers sit through to a *sit-up* position, knees up and hands behind the head. We begin with 50 and add 2 a day until we reach 100. From the sit-up, we go to *leg lifts*. The wrestlers lay flat on their backs with their hands behind their heads. On the command "up" they raise their legs 6 inches. On the command "apart" they spread their legs about 24 inches. The commands are repeated at various heights for about 60 seconds. Last of the one-man exercises are the *neck bridges*. Two minutes are allowed for bridging and spinning on the neck. As the neck strengthens, team members will pair off and each boy will bridge with his partner across his chest.

Two-man isometrics: Since the wrestlers are already lined up by weight, it is an easy matter to pair off in equal size for two-man isometrics.

> NOTE: After the wrestlers have assumed the proper position, the coach will start the exercise with a whistle, time 10 seconds with a stop watch, and stop the drill with a whistle. The wrestlers are then told to move to the next position.

Arm wrestle: Both wrestlers take a prone position facing each other and grasp right hands in Indian wrestling fashion (10 seconds). They then follow the same procedure using the left hand (10 seconds).

Pushing: The wrestlers, still facing each other, come to a kneeling position and interlace the fingers of both hands (10 seconds).

Pulling: The wrestlers now assume a sitting position, place their feet against their partners with the knees up, and grasp wrists (10 seconds).

Leg lifts: One wrestler will lie on his back while his partner, kneeling, will grasp his ankles and anchor them to the floor. The bottom man will fight this resistance in an attempt to lift his legs off the mat (10 seconds).

Leg spreads: From the same position, the bottom man will attempt to spread his legs (10 seconds).

Legs together: This exercise is performed from almost the same position as the leg spread exercise. But instead of the legs being together, the wrestler spreads them about 18 inches and attempts to bring them together against the resistance of his partner (10 seconds).

Two-man exercises: After isometrics, the wrestlers stay with their partners for 3 additional exercises designed primarily to strengthen the neck and stomach.

Bridge headstand: From a bridging position (stomach up), the wrestler reaches over his head and grasps the ankles of his partner who is standing 12 inches from his head. The bridging wrestler then kicks hard, arches his back, and pulls with his arms until he reaches a headstand position. The legs are then opened to: (a) straddle the standing partner; (b) both legs to the right side of the standing partner; (c) both legs to the left side of the standing partner.

> NOTE: All during the exercise, the hands remain holding onto the standing partner's ankles and the weight of the exercising wrestler is on his neck. The exercise is completed by returning to the original position of the neck bridge.

Two-man sit-ups: In the two-man sit-ups, the wrestler's partner takes an all-fours referee's position on the mat. The wrestler performing the exercise straddles his partner, placing his toes under the hands of his partner. The top man then leans back until his head touches the mat. He then returns to the original position, using his stomach muscles to pull himself up.

> NOTE: After completing the desired number of sit-ups, the wrestler reverses his position on top so that he is straddling his partner and now is facing his partner's feet. The top man then hooks his feet inside of his partner's thighs. He bends back to touch his head to the mat and returns to the starting position to complete his sit-up.

Body stand: For the body stand exercise, the bottom man again takes the down referee's position. The top man moves to a position perpendicular to him. The top man then hooks one arm around his partner's arm and the other under his partner's stomach. He then pulls and kicks high to a body stand. The top man continues to arch until his feet touch the mat on the opposite side of his partner. By pulling back, he can return himself to the body stand and then continue back to his original position.

Running: Weather permitting, we next take a one- or two-mile run over our cross-country course. The wrestlers are asked to bring running shoes to school so as not to damage their wrestling shoes. Time can be kept for the run and a standard set. Sometimes, we set a minimum time for the one-mile run, say 6:45, and anyone who fails to make that time or under must run another mile.

> RUN IN-PLACE: When the weather doesn't permit outside running, we run in-place inside the wrestling room. We line up as in calisthenics and on command begin running in-place. The knees are kept waist high. We continue this for 50 seconds and then sprint an additional 10 seconds. This 60-second exercise can be repeated as often as you wish.

All of our calisthenics can be completed in about 30 minutes, if we limit running to one mile. Some may believe that this takes too much time from other aspects of your wrestling program—but we feel that it's time well spent. Since beginning this type of program, we have had very few injuries or lost practice time due to illness. Our wrestlers take a great pride in doing their calisthenics, especially when we periodically increase the number or repetitions. They feel that because they work harder and are in better shape than their opponents, they have a better chance of winning.

5

Wrestler's 3-Point Conditioning Program

by Mike Koval

**Head Wrestling Coach
Hiram College
Hiram, Ohio**

In his last five years as head wrestling coach at Hiram College, Mike Koval has built this impressive record: 50-4-1, four Ohio Athletic Conference crowns (team was runner-up the fifth year), and at least one individual champion each year.

Wrestler's 3-Point
Conditioning Program

At Hiram College, we divide our physical conditioning program for wrestlers into three distinct periods: 1) preliminary conditioning (isometrics, weights, running and calisthenics); 2) pre-season conditioning (isometrics, running, calisthenics and wrestling drills); 3) regular season conditioning (drills, correcting match mistakes, and advanced techniques).

> COMBINATION: To save time, we teach skills in the form of drills. This way, the boys learn how to wrestle while they are getting stronger. For example, we seldom drill just for conditioning (running in place, hit the mat, and so on). Instead, we use a drill like the following: *Takedown drill*—drop and spin in position on one hand outside opponent's knee—return to start—repeat drill to opposite side. These combined "skill-drills" take up 75% of our program.

Here is what we do at each of the three stages of our program.

Preliminary conditioning: This part of our program starts on or about October first and lasts for one month. It consists of isometrics, weight training, running and calisthenics. Mondays, Wednesdays and Fridays are taken up with running and isometrics while Tuesdays and Thursdays are devoted to weights and calisthenics.

I believe that light enough weights should be used so that the lifter can accomplish rapid repetitions (6 to 8 per exercise). The principle involved here is to strive for speed using the overloading theory.

Many isometric exercises are used today and they can be obtained from a variety of sources. Listed below are several exercises that we use which incorporate most of the principles of isometrics.

Crushing exercise: (Diagram 1.) The wrestler's arms should be head high. He should then pull the dummy against his shoulder in a crushing or hugging movement. This exercise will develop the muscles on the front of the arms and chest.

Shin press (foot flexor): (Diagram 2.) Partner holds the upper surface of the feet in his hands and prevents the athlete from flexing his foot. This exercise will strengthen the muscles in front of the leg and will reduce the incidents of shin splints, sprained ankles, and foot arch trouble.

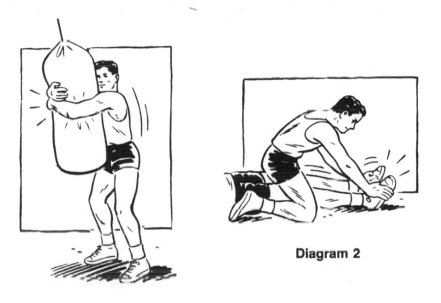

Diagram 2

Diagram 1

Leg curl: (Diagram 3.) This is a special exercise used to insure development of the hamstrings. The athlete lies on the ground, face down, as shown in the diagram. He then pushes up with his foot against pressure.

The emphasis in all weight and isometric exercises should be on the development of the arms and legs.

Diagram 3

RUNNING: We feel that running is an extremely important part of conditioning. It is an excellent leg-builder, develops endurance, increases lung capacity and is vital for giving wrestlers that "second wind" which is often the difference between winning and losing. A bonus value: many wrestlers find that running is the secret to weight reduction.

All October running should be done outside either on the cross-country course or on the track. During the first week, one mile of running combined with some sprinting and jogging is adequate. For the second week, the wrestlers should run two miles with some sprinting and jogging. By the third week of the month, the team should be worked up to a three-mile run and some sprinting and jogging each day. We have found that running tends to become boring for the boys. In order to decrease the boredom, we add some spice to the running part of our program by having the boys run for time against the watch, having them run with different teammates and by occasionally running the lettermen against the freshmen.

NOTE: Daily "preliminary conditioning" should not exceed 45 minutes. The squad should learn to run through isometrics and weights precisely and briskly and do their running quickly. There must be no loafing during workout sessions.

Pre-season conditioning: We start pre-season conditioning around November 1 (this is usually four weeks prior to our first meet). It consists of running, isometrics, calisthenics, and drills. Here is a time breakdown of each:

Isometrics—15 minutes three days each week.
Calisthenics—10 minutes of strenuous exercises each day.

Demonstrations—5 minutes each day.
Drills—60 minutes each day.

Since drills take up the majority of the wrestler's practice time, it is easily understood why skills must be incorporated into them. The skills should be selected carefully to fit in with the philosophy of the coach. By this I mean that if a coach believes (as I do) in teaching 90% offense and 10% defense, he should choose drills that incorporate offensive skills almost entirely.

NOTE: As in our preliminary conditioning program, the boys run three miles each day. The three miles are also run daily in our regular season program.

Regular season conditioning: Once the season begins (usually on or about December 1), we continue with our isometrics and running. Less time, however, is devoted to these parts of the program and we concentrate mainly on perfecting skills, developing speed and learning advanced techniques. Some time is also spent learning special moves in preparation for our next opponents. The procedure for teaching new moves is as follows. Once the maneuver is introduced to the squad and learned by them, it is repeated as fast as possible without sacrificing correct execution. This type of speed drilling teaches a learned skill or reaction which is conducive to lightning type reflexes that are necessary to outmaneuver an opponent.

Supplementary neck conditioners: Because I believe that proper neck development is absolutely essential for the wrestler, we use the two following "buddy" drills throughout the season. Of course, we also use the "standard" exercises (plain bridge, and so on).

Drill 1: Wrestler No. 1 jumps astride his buddy, scissoring his legs around buddy's waist and clasping his hands around his neck as illustrated in Diagram 4. Wrestler No. 2 (the "buddy") bends forward and straightens up alternately. No. 1 moves his hands higher on No. 2's neck with each repetition. We like to have the boys work up to 20 repetitions by the end of the season.

Drill 2: Wrestler No. 1 is in a back bridge and No. 2 stands facing him at arm's length. No. 1 pulls himself into a head stand by holding on to No. 2's ankles for support. He then lets himself down to the original bridge position. The sequence is repeated 8 to 10 times. (Diagram 5.)

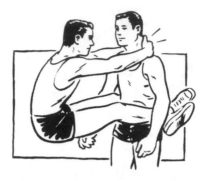

Diagram 4

Diagram 5

6

Developing a Strong Grip in Wrestling

by Bill Archer

Head Wrestling Coach
Huntington High School
Huntington, West Virginia

Bill Archer has been head wrestling coach at Huntington High School for the past six years, leading his teams to five regional titles and a 43-4 record. Coach Archer is himself a former state champion wrestler at Huntington High.

Developing a Strong Grip
in Wrestling

The strength of a wrestler's grip is probably one of the most often overlooked areas in wrestling.

Most coaches have their wrestlers do fingertip push-ups in addition to their normal wrestling, and that's about it for grip-strength work.

We at Huntington High School have come to believe that the strength of a wrestler's grip is very important, and use the following program to develop it to the fullest.

First, we explain to our wrestlers the importance of grip strength.

We emphasize that good grip strength will greatly add to their ability to control or take down an opponent, and we remind them that the Russians have long been noted for their rope climbing and grip work.

SEVEN EXERCISES

1. Running: We do almost all of our running with the wrestlers carrying and squeezing rubber balls. Also, we have our wrestlers carry weight plates (on their fingertips, of course) as they run.

2. Rope climbing: We climb ropes every day after practice. It's useful to have the wrestlers race or to time them. You can also use ropes for the conventional tug-of-war.

3. Wrist curls: From the seated position, drop your wrists over your knees and curl weights the full range of wrist movement. Twenty-five repetitions.

4. *Fingertip push-ups:* Regular push-ups, but up on fingertips.

5. *Finger snaps:* Wrestlers stand with arms extended. They open and close their hands in quick succession. This is an excellent exercise.

> NOTE: And it gives the coach a chance to do an exercise with his team and not get out of breath!

6. *Wrist rolls:* With the conventional weight-training wrist roller, you can use any number of exercises. We've found that standing with the arms extended is the best position.

7. *Fingers tug-of-war (Figure 1):* Both wrestlers drop down to the position they would use for bent-knee sit-ups. They place the balls of their feet together and lock fingers. Each attempts to pull the other off the mat. Both men lose if contact is broken.

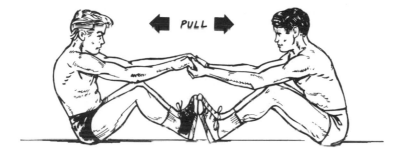

Figure 1

Part VI

Wrestling Drills

1

Pin Drills
for Inexperienced Teams

by Tim Lull

Head Wrestling Coach
Deshler High School
Tuscumbia, Alabama

Tim Lull's record as head wrestling coach at Deshler High School is 14-6-1. The Deshler Tigers finished ninth in the 1974 Class AAA State Tournament and second in 1975, producing a pair of all-American grapplers along the way. In addition, the Tigers have finished in the top three in six of the nine tournaments in which they've participated.

Pin Drills for Inexperienced Teams

On taking the job as head wrestling coach at Deshler High School, I had to determine a philosophy of wresting—for a team that had never even seen a match.

This philosophy had to apply to each individual wrestler's ability to score enough bout points in order to win the match.

The difficulty lay in the fact that the vast majority of our opponents had experience and we had none.

If we could win one bout by a pin, our opponents would have to win at least two by a decision to stay even.

To win by a pin and not get pinned ourselves was the only way that we could possibly compete with our experienced opponents.

Thus, our team philosophy was determined—*Pin 'Em!*

NOTE: Can you imagine trying to convince a first-year wrestler that he can pin the self-confident, experienced man on the opposite side of the mat?

I knew in reality that pinning would be difficult in most bouts and impossible in others. Still, scoring from pinning combinations was the only way we could win bouts, and consequently matches.

Two ideas backed me up on this. First, near-fall points could add up to a major decision. Second, the bottom man's exertion from bridging could wear him out to the point that he might be pinned.

WHAT TYPE OF PINNING COMBINATIONS?

Through research into wrestling, I decided on the type of pinning combinations that we would use.

I found that 95 per cent of all pins are achieved with the half-nelson, or some combination of the half-nelson.

Therefore, the half-nelson and the reverse half-nelson became our primary pinning combinations, followed by the cradle series.

After researching the pin moves to be used, the next step was to determine exactly how to teach the moves.

NOTE: The number of pinning combinations a wrestler knows is not nearly as important as the number he can apply.

The most significant aspect involved is that the wrestler must know when each pinning move is needed. The correct selection could result in a near-fall or a pin; wrong selection could result in no points or a reversal.

PIN DRILLS

Through pin drills, our wrestlers were put into situations where a selection had to be made.

The following drills are the most successful that have evolved from our practices. These and other pin drills are scheduled for 10 minutes every day.

This 10-minute period has proven to be the most rewarding area of our practices.

NOTE: Over the past two years, our drills have helped us win more than 60 per cent of our matches by pins and score three near-falls for every one by our opponents.

Remember, most bouts are decided by close scores. Even though a pinning situation may not achieve a fall, bout points awarded for the near-fall can give a wrestler a decided advantage in a close match.

HALF-NELSON DRILLS

Because the half-nelson is the most frequently used combination, it is important that every wrestler know how to change to other combinations from the half-nelson.

Thus, the majority of our drills involve switching to and from the half-nelson and reverse half-nelson.

Drill one: Begin with one man on his back (B) and the other on top (T), with a half-nelson crotch.

B turns away from T. As T feels the half-nelson slipping out, this point must be recognized as "change time." To change from the half to the reverse half, the wrestler must do three things:

(1) Drag his elbow across B's face, trying to wipe off his nose.
(2) Slide his hand around the top of B's head.

NOTE: If the hand, rather than the elbow, goes across B's face, there's a hole of about 1 foot through which B can shoot his hand, since most forearms are about 1 foot from wrist to elbow.

(3) Grab B's far armpit hard, thus completing the reversal.

To return to the half-nelson, B turns toward T's waist. As T begins to lose his reverse half, he again:

(1) Drags his elbow across B's nose.
(2) Slips his hand around B's head.
(3) Finishes by sliding the hand between his own and B's chest.

Many times, while in a half-nelson pin situation, we found ourselves being forced toward B's head, ending up parallel and missing precious back points. Another drill was needed.

Drill two: Start in the half-nelson crotch position, with B turning away from T. "Change time" begins as the near arm of the bottom man is starting to work free.

With the crotch hand, T hooks the near arm down through the armpit, simultaneously moving toward B's head.

T is now on both knees at B's head, with a deep half-nelson and one arm hooked.

As B bridges and turns, T fights the pressure. When B turns into T, T turns his head in that direction and places the side of his head on B's chest, applying pressure down.

Drill three: Beginning in the half-nelson crotch position, B bridges up and turns into T, trying to shoot his outside arm between their chests.

NOTE: Many wrestlers refuse to release the crotch and end up losing valuable back points.

"Change time" occurs as this arm starts reaching for the chest.

Using the crotch hand, T hooks B's far arm down under the armpit.

Upon achieving this under hook, he throws his elbow as high toward B's head as possible. This stretches out B's arm, forcing his shoulder toward the mat.

CRADLE DRILLS

Through trial and error, we found that we could cradle a man from almost any position on the mat.

The easiest way to pin a man is to let him put himself in the pin position and then hold him there.

Drill one: Start with B broken down on his belly.

There are now only two directions in which B should work in order to return to his base. If he works his outside knee up, T sticks in the cross-face cradle.

NOTE: An important point about the cross-face cradle is that a man's legs are stronger than his arms. In the cross-face cradle, you "stick your hip in his ear" and, with your legs, drive his head toward his legs until you can lock up.

If B works up with his inside leg, T reaches over B's head and grasps his near armpit. He grabs through the crotch from the rear with the other hand, sticks his head in B's side, and locks his hands to complete the inside cradle.

Next, in the base position, B performs four moves from which T can cradle him: (1) sit out, (2) switch, (3) inside stand-up, and (4) outside stand-up.

As B executes these moves, T moves directly into either an inside or an outside cradle.

NOTE: A man can be put into a cradle from anywhere, *if* the top man will maintain "pressure down."

While preparing to lock your hands and sit through with your legs, you must keep your weight on the back of the bottom man's neck, maintaining pressure down through the knees.

Drill two: Begin with B on his belly for two minutes, moving at half-speed and endeavoring to put T in as many cradle situations as possible.

As the skill level increases, the wrestlers can work at three-quarter speed.

NOTE: This drill takes four minutes of the 10 allotted for pin drills—two minutes in each position for each wrestler.

GENERAL PROCEDURE

Each drill is conducted in much the same way.

The wrestlers pair off and spend equal amounts of time in each position.

NOTE: Half-nelson drills usually last one minute in each position. Cradle drills are generally practiced for one and a half to three minutes in each position.

Performance in matches determines the frequency with which each drill is practiced.

CONCLUSION

Until these pin drills became a regular part of our program, we were just like any other team of inexperienced wrestlers.

We now have some experience, but our philosophy has not changed: We try to pin our man before he can beat us with his moves.

2

Chain Wrestling Drills

by Robert Halverson

**Head Wrestling Coach
Minico High School
Rupert, Idaho**

Robert Halverson has been head wrestling coach at Minico High School since 1961. His teams have an overall dual-match record of 137-8-1, with seven district championships, three Idaho state titles, and one state runner-up.

Chain Wrestling Drills

We believe that a wrestler, to be effective, must master a few fundamental moves in a chain or series. Thus, we employ five elementary drills that teach wrestlers the basic series in fundamental wrestling.

NOTE: Because of the large turnout and limited wrestling room space, we consolidated and carefully selected each drill to accomplish the most from each series.

When a boy masters the basic wrestling series, he can start adding to his repertoire.

Shooting against wall: We begin by having our wrestlers shoot against a cinderblock wall. All wrestlers must shoot within an area two blocks wide and four blocks high. They must always stand at the base of the wall.

COACHING POINTS: Stance; elbows in; arms shooting straight out; back straight; head up; palms flat; belly against wall; shoot with both left and right knee down.

Multiple techniques: The next drill covers many different techniques. We place one wrestler on his right knee and on the ball of his left foot—a position he would be in if he has shot against the wall. Another wrestler faces him an arm's length away.

On the whistle, both boys race across the wrestling room— wrestler down must stay down; the other wrestler runs backwards. From the down position, the wrestler can use the double-leg tackle, single leg, back heel, or ankle pickup.

COACHING POINTS (Using drill offensively): Elbows in; shoot

arms straight out; back straight; head into opponent's ribs; lift and pull opponent's leg into your body; ankle trip; quarter turn on knee, landing on a good base; come up quickly, head up, for a quarter-nelson pin.

COACHING POINTS (Using drill defensively): Reaction; sprawl; pancake spin; crossface (with possible cradle); counter double leg.

At first one wrestler may outrun the other. If this is so, then the one down is shooting too slow or is not carrying through and individual work on shooting is necessary.

TIPS: Do not use the drill as a combination, for it is designed to allow offensive or defensive coaching points. Using it as both discourages young wrestlers. There are several games that can be worked out, and you can make wrestling a lot of fun while working hard.

Football blocking dummy: For this drill we employ a foam rubber blocking dummy 4 feet high, 12 inches wide, and 6 inches thick. The wrestler facing the dummy assumes his attack stance and moves as if facing an opponent. The wrestler holding the dummy moves about as if he were going to attack.

The wrestler shooting sets up the wrestler holding the dummy and shoots. Upon contact, the dummy holder releases the dummy and the wrestler shooting carries through his moves completely. Coaching points include—stance; movement on attack; telegraphing moves; arms straight out; and most important, the setting up of the opponent.

NOTE: These three drills complete the series while on the foot. As you can see, one drill can accomplish several purposes, thus saving much needed time. Make your wrestlers work both left and right, using both left and right knee down and landing both ways. We believe that when you are on the bottom, constant movement is a must. We tell our wrestlers that if their butts are not moving, they are not moving.

Float drill. We use two basic drills from the down position that complete all our basic moves; the first is a float drill. One wrestler is down, the other in position on top. We tell the top man not to block or pin but just ride and counter, staying on top.

The bottom man works on his basic moves—side switch, turn under, sit out, switch, turn under, inside switch, stand-up switch.

COACHING POINTS (Top man): Balance; not too high; mouth shut; carriage of head; control of opponent's head; throwing of feet and legs; throw down from behind; counters.

COACHING POINTS (Bottom man): Keep the rear end moving; control of arms; head up; off of your belly or side; make more than one move in the series.

We start this drill with 30-second periods and four periods: #1 on top right side, #1 on bottom, #1 on top left side, #1 on bottom. We stress working from both the left and right sides. If a reversal occurs, he immediately starts down again, wasting no time beginning again.

Blindfold drill: This is our most popular drill. We blindfold the bottom wrestler. We do this because we believe that a wrestler must be able to feel, not see his moves, and to balance and counterbalance. In the more advanced drill, we blindfold both wrestlers.

COACHING POINTS: The bottom man, blindfolded, soon realizes that he must be in constant motion. He must plan his attack with the basic reversals and not make a mistake. The top man soon realizes he must use his balance—also, he soon learns the hazards of not countering properly. He must sense his opponent's move instead of waiting for it to hit him too late.

We allow the blindfolded wrestlers to go two minutes or until a pin occurs. We also allow the wrestlers to fight off the back. They work on their own blindfolded, because it points up weaknesses in the their wrestling. They do not have to be told.

Conclusion: The five basic sets or series of drills we use fit our style of wrestling. By using your imagination, you can work these drills into situations and positions—and still have a little fun with the work involved.

3

Skill Drills for Execution and Conditioning

by Gordon Churchill

Head Wrestling Coach
Sky View High School
Smithfield, Utah

Gordon Churchill has been coaching at Sky View for the past five years and has been head wrestling coach for the past two. His overall record is 115-31-3 and includes six regional championships. In the past two years his record was 54-12. Coach Churchill has coached two state champions.

Skill Drills for Execution
and Conditioning

We attribute much of our success in wrestling to the drills we use; they are as close to actual wrestling as possible. We do most of these drills daily to perfect skills and execution. They also serve to loosen up the wrestler and condition him. Here are a few of them.

SWITCH DRILL

The wrestler starts out in the referee position (Photo 1A). On the whistle, he will pivot on his right foot and kick his left foot through and underneath his right leg, being careful not to let his rear-end touch the mat. At the same time, he brings his right elbow down hard (Photo 1B). Then, without stopping, he continues back up into the referee position and pivots on the left foot, kicking the right foot through and under the left leg—again not touching his rear-end and bringing the elbow down hard (Photo 1C).

NOTE: This is done for 1 or 2 minutes at full speed. It's designed to help teach the switch for those of us who still like the skill.

SIT-OUT

The wrestler starts out in the referee position (Photo 2A). On the whistle, he can perform several skills. Photo 2B shows the wrestler doing a switch continuously moving. Photo 2C shows

Photo 1A

Photo 1B

Photo 1C

Photo 2A

Photo 2B

Photo 2C

him doing a sit-out and then moving into a standing switch (Photo 2D).

> NOTE: The drill is done for 1 or 2 minutes and teaches constant motion and chain wrestling.

BALANCE DRILL

The bottom wrestler starts out in the referee position. The top wrestler puts his chest on the bottom wrestler's lower back (Photo 3A) and places his hands out to his sides. He cannot allow his knees to touch the mat while performing this drill. This teaches the top wrestler to make the bottom wrestler carry his weight and also balance on him. On the whistle, the bottom man moves, performing either a sit-out or switch (Photos 3B and 3C); the top man keeps his weight back and floats and balances on the bottom man. Neither wrestler can use his hands.

> NOTE: We do this drill for 1 or 2 minutes.

WALL T.D.

The wrestler stands arm's length from the wall in a good takedown position (Photo 4A). After a good setup (head fake, chin-tip, etc.), he shoots in on the wall, one knee down (Photo 4B), making sure his chest is against the wall, head up, back straight, elbows in. When the wrestler ends up in this position, he should lift, keeping the chest, hands, and arms against the wall and bringing his leg underneath him until he is in the standing position.

> NOTE: We do this drill for 5 or 10 minutes. It teaches the wrestler to be at about the right distance away from his opponent before shooting for a takedown. Also, it teaches him to keep his head up, back straight, and elbows in.

LEG PICKUP

The drill starts with both wrestlers in the referee position (Photo 5A). The top man picks up the bottom man's left ankle

Photo 2D

Photo 3A

Photo 3B

Photo 3C

Photo 4A

Photo 4B

(Photo 5B). The bottom man reaches down and grabs the top man's wrist and rotates his weight on and over the ankle, and can either push or pull the top man's hand off his ankle; the top man then jumps back to his left and picks up the bottom man's ankle again (Photo 5C), and the procedure is repeated.

> NOTE: We do this drill for 1 or 2 minutes. It teaches the top man to ride legs and the bottom man to wrestle that hand on the ankle.

FRONT BALANCE DRILL

This drill starts with one wrestler down on his knees, arms out to his side. The top wrestler puts his chest on the bottom wrestler's back and head (Photo 6A). On the whistle, the top man moves as fast and as hard as possible, trying to spin back and around the bottom wrestler. Going first to the right (Photo 6B) and then to the left (Photo 6C), the bottom wrestler counters the top wrestler's moves by spinning to his left and right as the top wrestler spins—and by bringing up his arm to the side the top wrestler is moving to. If the top man happens to get behind the bottom man, the bottom man should sit out and turn and should then be facing the top man again.

> NOTE: The drill teaches the top man to balance on the bottom man, and the bottom man to keep moving. It also teaches the bottom man quickness and to keep the top man in front of him. We do the drill for 1 or 2 minutes.

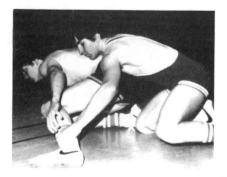

Photo 5A   **Photo 5B**

Photo 5C

Photo 6A

Photo 6B

Photo 6C

STAND-UP DRILL ON WALL

The drill starts with the wrestler down in the referee position, his back to the wall, his toes touching or close to the wall (Photo 7A). On his own, the wrestler should explode backward toward the wall, either bringing up his inside or outside foot. Grabbing the hand that will be on his stomach, he should drive the other elbow backwards hard into the wall with palm facing up to clear opponent from him (Photo 7B). Wrestler should keep his back straight and head up at all times.

Photo 7A   **Photo 7B**

NOTE: We do this as many times as possible within the 2 to 5 minutes allotted for the drill. It teaches the proper stand-up method and assures perfection of the skill.

4

Combination Skill Drills

by Arnold W. Umbach

Former Head Wrestling Coach
Auburn University
Auburn, Alabama

Arnold W. Umbach formed the first wrestling team at Auburn University in 1946. The first Southeastern Intercollegiate Wrestling Tournament was held in 1947 and Coach Umbach's teams won 20 of those titles. His record for dual meets at Auburn is 249-28-5. Arnold Umbach is a past president of the American Wrestling Coaches Association and a member of the Helms Hall of Fame and the NCAA Rules Committee. He is retired from active coaching.

Combination Skill Drills

We have had to do a number of things differently at Auburn University, since wrestling is rather new in this part of the country. Most of the boys who come to us don't have as much wrestling experience as the average university student. We have had to start off with a few basic moves from each position. This calls for carefully planned practices to insure that facilities and talents are not wasted. The time spent in the practice areas is often scarce because of the great demands made on students by an accelerated educational program. So this is where combination drills come in as great time-savers.

NOTE: Combination drills are two or more fundamental moves thrown together. They teach the wrestler to maintain good balance and control so he will be in position to make the next move quickly. They teach quick and natural reaction to each situation.

Example: When we have taught several escapes, reverses and counters from underneath and have drilled on them separately, we put two or more of these maneuvers together in one drill. The same thing is true with takedowns and other phases of wrestling. Let us use this situation for an example: Your opponent starts out with a *sit out,* and you counter with an *overdrag.* When you come on top, you are in a natural position for your opponent to *switch;* if he puts his arm around your waist, it would be natural for you to *counter switch.* In these drills, the wrestlers should put enough resistance in each move so that both will get a good feel of the hold.

ILLUSTRATIONS: In the illustrations that follow, wrestler A is distinguished by the dark outfit. Note that his hair, shoes and trunk are dark, while wrestler B is light in color. This will make it easier to distinguish one from the other when their feet, head and arms become entangled.

Offensive and defensive drills: Here is one of our basic combination drills (sit out, overdrag, counter and switch). We start when the whistle blows with both wrestlers in referee's position on the mat in top and bottom positions. We use this drill from both sides.

Figure 1   **Figure 2**

Figure 1: Wrestler A is in the referee position underneath and wrestler B is in the top position to wrestler A's right.

Figure 2: A grabs B's left wrist with his left hand and brings his own left foot forward.

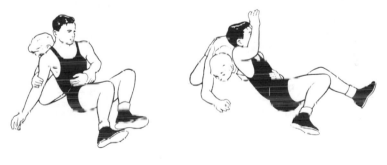

Figure 3   **Figure 4**

Figure 3: A then brings his right foot forward and sits out, putting pressure on B's left shoulder.

Figure 4: A fakes to his left, putting pressure on B's left shoulder.

Figure 5

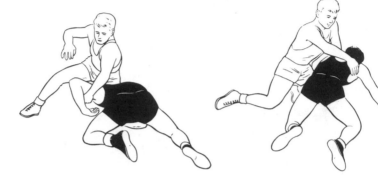

Figure 6   **Figure 7**

Figure 8   **Figure 9**

Figure 10   **Figure 11**

Figure 5: Then A turns back to his right and spins on his right shoulder. At the same time, B is getting his left hand in position to counter.

Figure 6: Note that as A pivots around on his knees, B has caught A's arm above his elbow for an overdrag.

Figure 7: B is now pulling A forward and at the same time springing behind A.

Figure 8: B is behind A, who has maintained good position for a counter, and has started a switch before B has complete control.

Figure 9: A pivots on his right foot and left hand, and swings out to his right to a sitting position.

Figure 10: A places his right hand in B's crotch and swings wide for more leverage, forcing B's right shoulder down.

Figure 11: A swings on behind and catches B in his crotch with his left hand, so that B cannot counter with a counter switch.

This is but one of our basic combination drills; there are many more. They teach the wrestler to be well prepared and alert for the next maneuver.

5

Drills for Conditioning and Skill Development

by Richard K. Collings

Head Wrestling Coach
West Grand High School
Kremmling, Colorado

Richard Collings has been coaching for six years—three of them at West Grand High School. His teams have compiled a 23-8 dual-match record, a league runner-up, a league championship, and a third-place state finish. He has also coached two state champions and a state runner-up.

Drills for Conditioning and Skill Development

The term "conditioning" is what our whole wrestling program is built around. We, like many small schools (140 students) involved in wrestling, have very limited facilities. We use the gymnasium or stage (both are small) as our main practice area. Here we can utilize only ⅔ of our mat, so we must use our area to the best of our ability. The term "our" refers to a very capable assistant, Coach Bob Dell.

NOTE: We have averaged 20 to 25 wrestlers per season, and a good test of our coaching ability has been to keep our wrestlers involved and working during all practice sessions, regardless of our practice area size.

Here are some of the things we do.

CONDITIONING AND ISOMETRIC DRILLS

We begin our season by a strict use of the conditioning drills, coordinated with skill learning achievement (skill learning achievement refers to the teaching of basic wrestling moves). We use the "buddy system," boys pair off according to size—then we use variations of isometric training, concentrating on the neck, groin, and hands.

Heading: This is moving the head in all four directions, separately—with reverse pressure from a buddy.

Leg pressure: (a) Lying flat, the boys raise the legs separately, with their buddy exerting opposite pressure. (b) Having the entire weight of the buddy placed on the foot of the knee bent to the chin, the wrestler lying flat pushes the buddy up and out.

Sit-ups: One buddy goes to the knee and hand position and the other buddy sits on the set wrestler's shoulders, with each buddy's legs interlocked. The top buddy proceeds to do sit-ups, by lengthening all the way backward to the mat with the head and coming up again.

NOTE: We stress that the bottom buddy push with his neck and head against the force of the top buddy.

Ball grab: Using a volleyball, we again place buddy pairs opposite each other—with the ball between them in their hands. They then try to pull the ball from their buddy's hands.

We concentrate on these isometric drills during the better half of the season. We also use many drills that condition the legs, wind, and endurance. The boys run stairs (three flights), sprints of 40 yards, and then jog and sprint laps. This running is done all through the season and has proven to be one of our better drills.

We have won a majority of our matches because our boys have been able to outlast opponents and thus defeat them. Our injuries have been held to a minimum—in three years, we have not had a serious injury. Also, all of our practice sessions end on a "run-in-place, hit-the-mat" sequence of eight minutes—hitting the mat at various timed intervals (emphasis being on hitting the chest and stomach).

EARLY-SEASON PRACTICE

A typical early-season practice session consists of the following:

1. Ten minutes of loosening up, calisthenics, jumping rope, use of a medicine ball, and occasionally a "tug-of-war."
2. Fifteen minutes of isometrics.
3. Thirty minutes of skill learning and development (actual wrestling and movement drills).

4. Ten minutes of running the stairs.

5. Eight minutes of 40-yard wind sprints.

6. Ten minutes of jogging and sprinting laps.

7. Five minutes of sit-out drills.

8. Five minutes of bear-walking (includes side-rolls and directional movements).

9. Ten minutes of review and application of techniques just learned.

10. Six to eight minutes of running and hitting the mat.

SKILL DRILLS

As the season moves along, we become more involved with the skill drills, which include both conditioning and skill development, but we never exclude the running drills. Some of our typical drills which involve conditioning and skill development follow.

Spin drill: Buddy system with same-size boys. One buddy in hands and knees position, the other buddy spins on top placing his weight over the shoulders of the bottom man. On the whistle the top man spins around, reversing directions and keeping well balanced. On the second whistle, the bottom buddy will sit-out and wrestle regardless of the top man's position. Intervals run 10 to 15 seconds.

Pinning drill: With one buddy flat on his back, the other buddy applies a pinning combination, and on a given whistle each tries to apply either the pin or the escape. Intervals are done at 20 seconds.

Rotation: By placing four pairs of wrestlers in our four corner areas of the mat, we begin in the referee's position and wrestle from a whistle for 45 seconds. Then the buddy at the disadvantage position moves clockwise on the next whistle and begins from the down position, with the next wrestler who won the advantage position. Our time limit for the drill is four minutes.

Group four: Wrestlers group themselves in four's according to size. One wrestler begins in the down position, as each of the other three wrestlers works for 30 seconds from the top position, separately. After the wrestler who started on the bottom has been worked by the other three wrestlers in his group, another wrestler takes his turn.

SUMMARY

The drills listed here are our main conditioning and skill achievement drills, which we supplement with other short drills and techniques. Throughout our drills, we discourage anything "fancy" and try to stick to good, sound, basic wrestling practice.

Our success over a three-year period, with our existing practice facilities, has been amazing. We have been fortunate enough to win several team and individual awards for our boys. They deserve them and some have received college notice and education.

6

A Progression Drill Program

by Jerry Halmrast

**Head Wrestling Coach
Bismarck High School
Bismarck, North Dakota**

Jerry Halmrast's career as a head wrestling coach at Bismarck High School spans four years. His teams are winners: four consecutive state team titles, eight individual state titles, and a 44-8-0 dual record.

A Progression Drill Program

Each fall at Bismarck, we are faced with the same problem that many wrestling coaches throughout the country have: a turnout of *inexperienced,* but eager wrestling hopefuls. We have to turn each boy's potential talent into actual talent. And we have to do it fast. Our approach to this problem has been to devise a system whereby we can "mass produce" wrestlers by developing a maximum of "wrestling sense" in a minimum of time. To do this most effectively with a large number of inexperienced boys, we concentrate during early season practices on our three phase progression drill program. It is divided into continuity, series and situation drills. Here is what we do.

DEMONSTRATIONS: Before we can use our continuity drills, we must first teach the basic maneuvers which will later be adapted to these drills. It is important for the new wrestler to know what end result he is attempting to achieve in a drill. For this reason, we have two of our most experienced wrestlers demonstrate a move at full speed. This shows the beginners what they will be trying for. Then, we have them demonstrate the same move in slow motion so that the inexperienced eye can see the different parts of the maneuver more easily.

After demonstrations, we break a maneuver down into its component parts and number each in sequence. We then drill "by the numbers" until the basic moves are learned. Following is an example of our count off technique used for the sit-out, turn-in, go-behind drill.

On command of: "ONE"—The defensive wrestler grasps opponent's wrist and tripods outside leg. "TWO"—Defensive wrestler thrusts his inside leg in front of him. "THREE"—He snaps over, coming to his knees. "FOUR"—He moves quickly behind opponent and gains control.

EFFECT: The count off method of teaching fundamental moves has proven to be most effective for me. It is the quickest way that I know of to teach a basic knowledge of moves to a beginner. Once they have this, they can progress to the first phase of our progression program.

CONTINUITY DRILLS

Although we call these drills "ten-second" drills, they may last longer. Their purpose is to allow each wrestler to repeat a certain maneuver a maximum number of times in a minimum amount of time, until the move comes naturally to him. The drills can be used or adapted to any wrestling maneuver that results in a reversal of advantage position. Resistance, of course, must be passive.

Sit-out, turn-in, go-behind: In this drill, the bottom wrestler completes the sit-out, turn-in and go-behind maneuver and, just as he gains control, his partner does the same maneuver. They continue this for ten seconds. As the boys become more proficient at the moves, they should be able to do them more rapidly and increase the number of repetitions in the allotted time.

Over-drag, reverse run-around counter: After the athletes are thoroughly familiar with the above drill, we coach them in this move. As the bottom man sits out and snaps over, the top wrestler hooks his hand under his partner's arm and quickly moves behind to regain control. The bottom wrestler then immediately starts a sit-out and turn-in from the opposite side. The top man continues to counter in the same way.

Switch and reswitch: The switch is probably the most readily adaptable move to a continuity type drill. Speed and form in execution, so necessary to all phases of wrestling, will rapidly improve through the daily use of this type of drill.

To adapt the switch and reswitch to a continuity drill, we do not allow the defensive wrestler to break the offensive wrestler completely to the mat. Instead, the defensive wrestler uses his leverage to swing up and behind to gain control while his opponent remains in position to execute a switch as soon as the defensive man gains control. As this move is mastered, we add the reswitch as a drill for countering the switch.

SERIES WRESTLING DRILLS

Once our wrestlers become proficient in the continuity moves, we begin to put continuity moves together so that they make sense in a wrestling context. There is no end to the number of combinations a coach can work out to adapt to this type of drill. Here is how we put some of ours together. Again, as in the continuity drills, resistance is passive.

Sit-out switch: The defensive man sits out and as he turns in, the top man counters with a chest spin and goes behind. The defensive man then immediately snaps into a switch in one continuous motion and gains control. Opponent then quickly repeats the same maneuver. They continue this for about ten seconds and then change positions to repeat the drill working from the opposite side.

Switch, reswitch, sit-out, over-drag and reverse run-around: The bottom wrestler begins to execute a switch and the top man counters with a reswitch. Bottom man then goes immediately into a sit-out and offensive wrestler counters with an over-drag and reverse run-around. Bottom man then quickly reacts going for a switch from the opposite side to start the whole series over again.

SITUATION DRILLS

Our situation drills are the final logical step in preparing new boys for competition. The continuity and series drills have provided the boys with a thorough knowledge of the basic wrestling moves and combinations. All that remains is to familiarize the wrestlers with the actual situations that they will face in competition. Here is how we do it.

Situation: We tell wrestlers, "You are tied with your opponent. There are ten seconds left in the match and you need an escape to win."

Drill: The boys are on the mat, one on offense and another on defense. On the whistle, they are told to wrestle. After ten seconds, we stop them and ask for a show of hands from the boys who were successful in gaining an escape.

Situation: Bottom wrestler is on his stomach and the offensive wrestler is allowed to get any breakdown or riding hold he wishes (they are not allowed to tie up both arms or legs).

Drill: On the whistle, they start to wrestle. The defensive man is given ten seconds to come up to a stable defensive position.

Situation: Defensive wrestler takes position on his back while offensive wrestler applies either a half or reverse nelson.

Drill: Defensive wrestler has ten seconds to get to his stomach. He must be especially careful to make sure that he does not allow both shoulders to be in contact with the mat for more than two seconds.